Making Gourd
Musical Instruments

W9-CRB-561

Making Gourd Musical Instruments

Ginger Summit & Jim Widess

Sterling Publishing Co., Inc.
New York

Library of Congress Cataloging-in-Publication Data

Summit, Ginger.

Making gourd musical instruments : over 60 string, wind &

percussion instruments, and how to play them / Ginger Summit, Jim Widess.

p cm.

Includes index.

ISBN 0-8069-1369 X

1. Musical instruments-Construction. 2. Gourds. I. Widess,

Jim. II. Title.

ML460.S94 1999

784.192'3-dc21   9911128

CIP

10 9 8 7 6 5 4 3 2 1

DESIGN BY LAURA HAMMOND HOUGH

Artwork on page 3 by David Roseberry, on page 6 by Marla C. Berns,

on page 8 (top) by Minnie Black and (bottom) Jerraldine Hansen

Published by Sterling Publishing Company, Inc.

387 Park Avenue South, New York, N.Y. 10016

© 1999 by Ginger Summit and Jim Widess

Distributed in Canada by Sterling Publishing

c/o Canadian Manda Group, One Atlantic Avenue, Suite 105

Toronto, Ontario, Canada M6K 3E7

Distributed in Great Britain and Europe by Cassell PLC

Wellington House, 125 Strand, London WC2R 0BB, England

Distributed in Australia by Capricorn Link (Australia) Pty Ltd.

P.O. Box 6651, Baulkham Hills, Business Centre, NSW 2153, Australia

Printed in China

All rights reserved

Sterling ISBN-13: 978-1-8069-1369-8 Hardcover

ISBN-10: 0-8069-1369-X

ISBN-13: 978-1-4027-4503-4 Paperback

ISBN-10: 1-4027-4503-6

We dedicate *Making Gourd Musical Instruments*

to our spouses, Roger Summit and Sher Widess,

for their inspiring love of music.

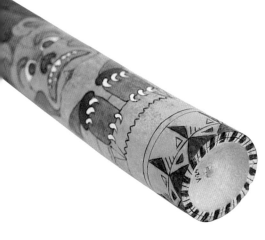

Contents

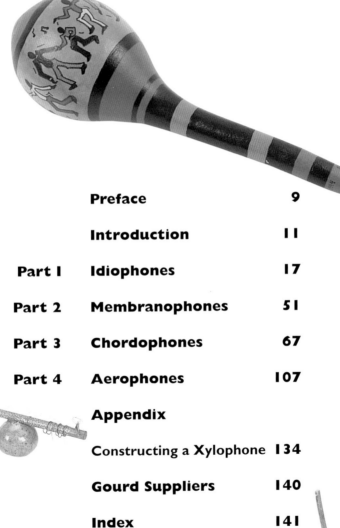

Preface

Almost everyone would like to make a musical instrument. You would like to, or you wouldn't have picked up this book and begun to read it. Most how-to-make-musical-instrument books require a vast workshop with expensive tools and serious woodworking or metal-working skills. Either that or the books are merely simple instruction manuals for making toy instruments from oatmeal or cigar boxes and use rubber bands or Popsicle sticks for strings or keys.

The most difficult part of a musical instrument to construct is the resonator: that part of the instrument where the distinctive sound really develops. Gourds are natural resonators—you don't have to do anything with a gourd but cut it open and clean it out. Presto, you have a banjo body, a drum frame, a bell for a wind instrument, or even a hollow tube for a flute.

Music appreciation goes back tens of thousands of years, when humans discovered that rhythmically beating on a hollow log, a stump, or another stick provided accompaniment for their voices in celebration or dance. Later, a seed pod or dried gourd may have added more sounds to singing and dancing around a fire.

While drying and stretching skins for garments or shelter, people learned that taut membranes could enhance the sound of a resonator. Then, with the invention of a bow and arrow, a whole new family of stringed instruments appeared.

It wasn't long before people discovered that hollow bones or stalks of grass made pleasant sounds when blown through. Holes in the tube added a whole new range of possibilities, giving multiple tones in one instrument.

The instruments in today's Western orchestra are very sophisticated—the quintessence of the instrument maker's art. To try to copy, let alone duplicate, these highly technically evolved instruments without the skill and tools necessary is daunting and fraught with disappointment.

In *Making Gourd Musical Instruments*, we step back and reconsider the development of playing music. Virtually every instrument played today has a gourd ancestor. Why, even the accordion has its roots in a 3,000-year-old Asian gourd instrument still played today, the *sheng*.

Using only the simplest tools found in almost every household, and odds and ends found in virtually every garage or garden shed, you can construct musical instruments from all the instrument families. These are serious instruments, tunable and playable, that you can be proud of and can perform on. In constructing and playing each one you will better understand the musical traditions that arose around its particular sound and capability.

As you explore each chapter and find exotic and unusual instruments, you will probably wonder what they sound like. We have produced an audio CD on which 30 of the instruments described in *Making Gourd Musical Instruments* can be heard. Ordering information can be found in the appendix.

We are indebted to many musicians and musicologists for their help in and support for our creation of *Making Gourd Musical Instruments,* among them: Andrew Tracey, from the International Library of African Music; J. Kenneth Moore, of the Metropolitan Museum of Art; Bart Hopkin, from Experimental Musical Instruments; Darrel Devore; Uli Wahl; Rimona Gale; Chris Johnson; Merle Teel; Geof Morgan; Robert Thornburg; Cliff Walker; Arthur Stephens; Salih Qawi; Randy Raine-Reusch; David Gamble. A special thanks to Bart Hopkin, Deborah Moskowitz, and Leland Bartholomew for reading the manuscript in its many forms. Many thanks also to Shelly, Roberto, Peeta, and Jenny, the staff at The Caning Shop, for giving us the time to do our work. Thanks go to the numerous musicians and artists who have shared their successes and failures with us.

Only humans make music for the sheer pleasure of making music.

Living is about learning and then sharing what we learn.

Introduction

Getting Started with Gourds

One of the most surprising things about gourds is their incredible variety of shapes and sizes. This is part of the reason they have been used for so many different kinds of instruments around the world.

When selecting a gourd for your musical project, the first criteria will be the size and shape. Pick up the gourd and examine it thoroughly. Look for a solid symmetrical shell that does not have obvious damage from bugs or disease. The actual thickness of the shell is not as important as the density—it should be firm when you press or tap it, since musical instruments are frequently beaten, shaken, or held under tension.

To test the gourd to see if it is completely dry, shake it and listen for the seeds or inner pulp to rattle. Then soak the dried gourd in water for 15 minutes, and use a metal kitchen scrubber to clean the mildewed outer skin. Draw a line on the shell with chalk or pencil where you want to cut it. The location of the cut line will vary depending on the type of instrument and gourd. Use a kitchen or hobby knife to make an initial opening in the shell along the line you have drawn. Any saw designed to cut wood is suitable for cutting a gourd. A keyhole saw or small hobby saw may be the best choice for cutting along a curved or irregular line.

Once the gourd is opened, remove the seeds and pulp. Wear a dust mask during this process. Any scraping tool, such as a serrated spoon or ceramic scraper, can be used for this job. Once all the pulp is removed, use coarse sandpaper to smooth the interior surface. The density of gourd shells varies, but the soft and porous inner shell absorbs sound vibrations. You can coat the interior with one or more coats of sealer, varnish, or polyurethane finish to minimize this effect. Sand

When completely dry, the gourd will usually be covered by mold and flaking skin, which must be removed before the gourd is crafted.

Put the gourd into a tub filled with warm water and cover it with wet towels. After the gourd has soaked for 15 minutes, the gourd skin is easy to remove with a stainless steel pot scrubber.

between each coat to get a smooth surface. Once the sealant is dry, you can proceed with your project. If the gourd shell cracks as you are working, it can be repaired with wood glue. If the crack is in a place that can be reached easily, you may want to reinforce it with a strip of silk cloth glued to the back as a support, like a bandage.

Some instruments, such as a vessel flute, have only a small opening drilled into one end of the gourd, which makes the cleaning of the insides difficult. One technique is to drill a hole of the appropriate diameter and then use a bamboo skewer or metal coat hanger to twist and break up the interior pulp. Shake the gourd and remove as much of the seeds and pulp as possible. Then fill the gourd with warm water and allow it to soak for several days. Pour out the water. Repeat this process several times until the gourd seems clean. Add rough gravel to clean any stubborn pulp and also to smooth the interior shell. Once the inside is cleaned, allow it to dry completely before you proceed to make the instrument.

Test the instrument as you proceed. If you're not pleased with the sound, it might be that the gourd you've chosen is not thick enough, or is too thick for the particular volume or resonance you need. Try a different gourd!

Once your musical instrument is completed, the gourd shell can be finished with many different materials and techniques. Products that can be used on paper, leather, or wood are also suitable on gourds. For a plain finish, use wood or leather polishes or stains, varnishes, or waxes, or oil polishes recommended for furniture. You may want to embellish the instrument with more ornamentation. Look at some of the examples in this book, or refer to a book on gourd craft for further ideas. (See *The Complete Book of Gourd Craft*, by Ginger Summit and Jim Widess.)

A (Very) Brief Review of Some Basic Acoustic Principles

Two different perspectives exist from which to examine sound—the way it is made, and the way it is perceived, or heard. The study of each of these topics can be very technical, and not within the scope of this book. But in making musical instruments, some principles need to be described, for they help explain not only how and why an instrument is made the way it is, but also how you can modify the completed project to get just the sound you want.

Sound is made by a series of vibrations that, once set in motion, expand and compress the medium in which they are traveling, such as air or water. When the vibrations hit the eardrum of the listener, they are transmitted through the middle and inner ear to the nerves of the brain, which perceives them as sound. The human ear can perceive waves that vibrate as slowly as 20–20,000 cps (cycles per second), although age and damage to the ear can reduce this range considerably. The main characteristics of the wave are how fast it is vibrating (frequency, which is perceived as pitch) and how large it is (amplitude, which is perceived as loudness). Some sounds are perceived as "noise," while others are "musical." (This is another topic for the physics book, although people from one generation or culture hear the music of another group of people as "just plain noise!") A musical note has one main vibration, which is the fundamental that distinguishes the pitch, and a series of secondary vibrations or waves above the fundamental, which are the overtones or harmonics. These determine the timbre, or tone color, of the perceived note. Noise, on the other hand, is a jumble of mixed vibrations with no identifiable pitch. Percussion instruments, such as rattles, generally produce "controlled noise" rather than specific pitches.

Some of the different ways a sound wave can be initiated are by striking, tapping, plucking, bowing, and even blowing against an object. In musical instruments, once the wave is initiated the body of the instrument either damps out or reinforces selected harmonics or overtones. In this way, the ear can perceive the difference between a note produced by a guitar, a xylophone, or a flute.

These principles will be elaborated further throughout this book as musical instruments are described. It is important to keep in mind that each gourd is unique in size, shape, shell thickness, and density. Therefore, it may be very difficult to get precise tones, scales, or harmonics from your instrument. If you work with the variability of the gourd, you will be rewarded with an instrument that has a unique and satisfying sound.

Instrument Categories

It is always difficult to come up with categories that work for a wide variety of objects, and that is especially true for systems that describe musical instruments. The first problem is to decide just exactly what constitutes a musical instrument. It is one thing to define instruments within a specified culture, but quite another when you want to include instruments from around the world and from earliest times. In 1914, Eric von Hornbostel proposed a very broad description: Everything counts as an instrument that makes sound intentionally. So then, how can this incredible array of objects be organized?

For the ancient Chinese, the science of music was based on the concept that instruments and the sounds they produced were directly related to the cosmic forces. Music and the understanding of musical instruments was so important to the well-being of politics and society that a separate cabinet post led by a minister of music was part of the imperial court. Instruments were divided into eight categories, based on the materials that either produced the sound or contained the vibrating air. These categories were: bamboo, wood, silk, clay, metal, stone, skin, and gourd. The most notable instrument in the "gourd" category was the *sheng,* which uses the gourd as a wind chamber.

A system used in India and Southeast Asia had four classes determined by the vibrating component: *tata vadhya* (stretched strings), *avanadha vadhya* (covered drums), *sushira vadhya* (hollow or pierced pipes), and *ghana vadhya* (solid objects, especially metal).

The system that most people in Europe and North America today are familiar with was based on a similar notion: woodwinds, brass, strings, and percussion. However, the names for these categories are very confusing, since they no longer describe the instruments within each group. Also, the criteria for classifying the instruments were inconsistent from the very beginning, and this problem has only increased as new instruments are introduced. Although these terms are familiar, they do not work well even for instruments in North America and Europe, and certainly not for the broad range of instruments found around the world.

A system that is widely used today by musicologists and is used for this book was created in 1914 by two German organologists—Curt Sachs and Eric von Hornbostel. It has undergone some modification since it was first proposed, but generally the system works well as a way to describe and understand instruments from around the world. The Sachs-Hornbostel system, as it is known, is based on four broad classifications. Each is subdivided into several subclassifications, which in turn are divided still further to include all possible variations. The system is based on the criterion, *What is the nature of the vibrating body?* The four basic categories are:

- Idiophones: The initial vibrator is solid material that vibrates by virtue of its own rigidity.
- Membranophones: The initial vibrator is a stretched membrane, such as a drum skin.
- Chordophones: The initial vibrator is a stretched string.
- Aerophones: The initial vibrator is air, either enclosed in a chamber or free.

This system has been adopted and used as a standard by musicologists around the world. But there are many instruments that don't fit neatly into one category, such as the harp-lute (*kora*) or plucked drum (*gopiyantra*). In this book we have tried to follow the conventional groupings established by the Sachs-Hornbostel system, as much as possible.

Historically, gourds have been used to make instruments that belong in all these categories. For some instruments, gourds were gradually replaced by other materials, such as wood or metal. Instruments, after all, were constructed of materials that were handy in the immediate environment, and were modified as technology and materials became available. In some cases, such as the pierced fiddle or the *sheng/sho* (pipes in China and Japan), the more primitive forms that use gourds in their construction are still popular as folk instruments, while more formal adaptations are made with elaborately carved wood, ivory, and metal.

Gourds are still valued in the construction of many instruments even though other materials are also available, since gourds provide many unique sound qualities. Examples of this are found in many stringed instruments, including the banjo. There are other instruments for which gourds traditionally have not been considered a suitable material for construction, but because of the unique shapes gourds come in, they are being adapted to new uses, such as for flutes, clarinets, and even the Australian *didgeridoo*.

Today the versatility of the gourd is being enjoyed with renewed vigor. As you begin your musical adventure, there are a few requirements:

- Clean the gourd thoroughly before starting to make your instrument. Debris left in the gourd will interfere with the sound transmission, will dampen the volume, and will change the harmonics.
- Reinforce the shell with varnish, sealer, or other similar wood finish.
- Keep in mind that every gourd has its own characteristics, such as density, shell thickness, and shape, all of which affect the transmission of sound. Work with the small imperfections of the gourd as you find the voice of the instrument. You will be rewarded with a softness and smoothness of sound that is not possible with other material.

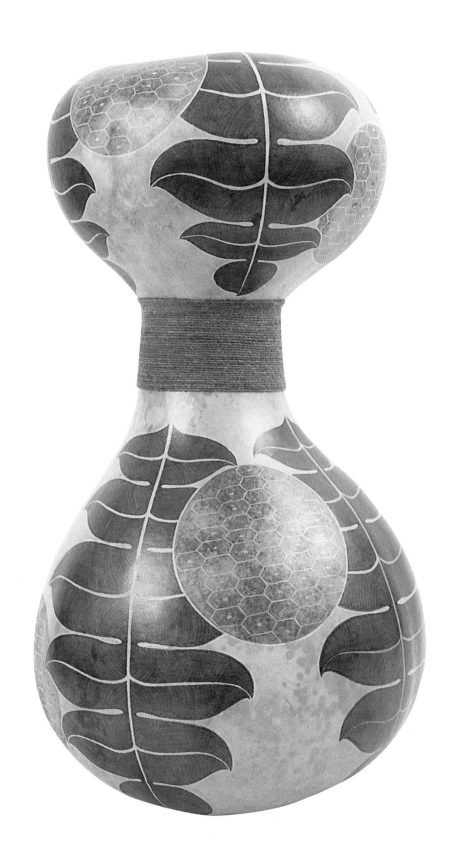

Part I

Idiophones

I diophones are among the oldest instruments used by humans. The term literally means self-sounding (*idio* = self, *phone* = sound). The body of the instrument itself is used to produce the initial vibration of sound, by virtue of its own rigidity. The sound source may be embellished with other resonators to enhance the sound, but it is the rigid body of the instrument, excited by such means as hitting, scraping, or plucking, which produces the original vibrations giving rise to the audible sound when transmitted to the surrounding air.

The category of idiophones is broad with numerous subcategories, based on how the instrument is played. Examples of instruments in each category include:

1. hit (simple)—sound bowl, water drum, gong
2. stamped—stamping tubes, *ipu heke*
3. shaken—rattles and *shekeres*
4. knocked together—*sistrum*
5. scraped—*guiro*/rasp
6. rubbed together
7 plucked—*mbira*
8. hit (complex)—xylophone

The first six subcategories of idiophones are basically percussion instruments. While they may be tuned to a general pitch range, in most cases these instruments are not intended to produce melody. However, the *mbira* and the xylophone can be tuned—some to 40 or more pitches.

While the body of the idiophone generates the sound by vibrating, the pattern of vibration depends on where and how the body is actually hit or struck. A solid object has a natural frequency at which it vibrates; the entire surface does not vibrate all at once or evenly. Some areas of the object will produce a maximum vibration, or sound wave, and others very little, because of the interaction of parts of the sound wave. Those areas that produce very little are called "nodes" and sound with a dull thud when struck. Therefore, to get the maximum sound, it is important to strike the body where the greatest vibration is produced. Different ways of holding or mounting the instrument body will have an effect on how the vibrations are transmitted or damped as well.

The mass of the body and the rigidity of the portion that will vibrate also determine the vibrating frequency of the idiophone structure, and therefore the pitch. The greater mass will lower the pitch (mass in this case refers not only to overall size but also the relative thickness of the shell or, in the case of the *mbira* or xylophone, the key of the instrument). The internal volume of the instrument affects the volume of sound resonated and the overtones that are reinforced, but not the initial pitch. If the parts that are to vibrate are more rigid, the pitch will be higher. Softer gourd shells will result in a lower tone.

It immediately becomes apparent that idiophones can range from the simplest of instruments to the extremely complex. They have certainly been used throughout the world, and most likely originated in many forms spontaneously and independently in cultures through the ages. Because gourds are relatively fragile and decompose rapidly, there are very few examples of ancient instruments that used gourds in their construction. However, by looking at pictures or etchings, reading historical descriptions, and observing the widespread use of gourds as idiophones throughout the world cultures today, it is reasonable to assume they played an important role in ancient instrument development and construction as well.

Hit (Simple)

Bowl

One of the simplest instruments that is still used informally in many cultures today is an overturned bowl. How many parents have let their children amuse themselves by taking all the kitchen bowls and pots from the shelves, turning them upside down, and becoming a noisy and energetic kitchen band?

In West Africa, calabash or gourd bowls are frequently overturned to become a type of percussion instrument:

- Several bowls may be placed in a line on a cloth or pad to become a tuned set. They are struck with either small gourd ladles or sticks.
- Frequently bowls are held against the chest, which becomes a secondary resonating chamber. By tapping the bowl with fingers that may have metal rings, the sounds can be varied and strong (referred to as a *horde* in Ghana).
- Occasionally men simply hold the inverted bowl between their knees. When the spontaneous music and social session is done, the bowls are returned to the kitchen or household.

Gourd tree *Courtesy of Harry Partch Archive, San Diego, California*
Photo by Danlee Mitchell

Wood Temple Gong

In many Southeast Asian countries, wooden temple gongs provide a tuneful resonance to musical ensembles. The powerful sounds they produce are largely a result of the hardwoods from which they are carved. A similar instrument can be created with hollowed gourds; although the sound will not be as loud, gourds can be cleaned and sealed to produce a wide range of tones. Be sure to select gourds with thick, dense shells for this project. These will produce a richer sound, and will also be less likely to crack when struck with a beater.

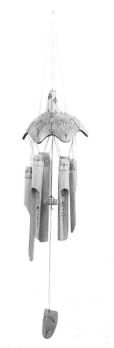

Three gourd gongs *Artwork by Ginger Summit*

Water Drum

Closely related to informal uses of the bowl as an instrument is the water drum, found in many cultures in West Africa as well as Meso America.

In many African tribes women are discouraged or forbidden from playing musical instruments, especially the sacred drums. So they have devised instruments using utensils from their own households. Two large washtubs or large gourds are placed next to each other and partially filled with water. Smaller gourd bowls are then floated upside down on the water surface and hit with mallets, usually a gourd ladle or spoon. The size and shape of the overturned bowl determines the pitch and overtones. Water drums are most often played by women within their own compounds for celebrations. At the end of the festivities, the instruments are returned to their more mundane daily functions. Now water drums are incorporated into many music groups, both formal and informal.

The water drum (also called *jicara de agua,* or *bubelek* among the Maya) is an important instrument in Meso America, where it is used to accompany dances, such as the deer dance, and celebrations among the native tribes. Occasionally a yoke or handle is attached to the container of water so the instrument can be played while the musician is standing or moving about. The inverted bowl may have a handle or cord attached to the side, so it can be raised or lowered while being played. Although any soft mallet will produce a strong tone, the Yaki of northern Mexico prefer a stick that has been wrapped with cornhusk and then bound with cord.

Bamboo wind chimes with gourd resonator
Artwork by Duane Teeter

Stamped

Another subcategory of idiophone produces vibrations by stamping a hollow instrument against a solid surface.

Water drums. The Mayan name is *bubelek.* Also used by the Yaki tribe in Sonora, Mexico, in the deer dance. *Artwork by Xavier Quijas Yxayotl*

Stamping Tubes

While one most frequently associates stamping tubes with long shafts of bamboo or hollowed sticks, gourds are also used. The women of the Ashanti tribe in Ghana and the Hausa in Nigeria have developed two such instruments that differ slightly in details of making and playing, but are quite similar in function. The *adenkum* stamp-

Shantu stamping tube from Nigeria *From the collection of Ginger Summit*

ing gourd made by the Ashanti women in Ghana is shaped like a club gourd or a thick medium-handled dipper gourd. The *shantu,* which is made by the Hausa in Nigeria, is an elongated snake gourd or other hardshell gourd with a long narrow neck that is thoroughly cleaned and embellished with woodburning.

To play this instrument, the performer sits cross-legged on the ground. With the left hand she taps the tube against the thigh, calf, open palm, shin, or even the ground. Another sound is produced by hitting the side of the gourd with the cupped hand or by slapping with the fingers. The right hand modulates various sounds by intermittently closing off the upper end of the tube.

Ipu Heke

In quite another part of the world, stamping drums were the exclusive domain of the men. In Hawaii, the *ipu heke* and the *ipu heke 'ole* are recognized as drums that accompany hula dancing; however, these instruments are not strictly drums—they are not constructed with a membrane, and the sound is produced by stamping them on the ground or on a pad and slapping them with the palm of the hand. Thus, they are properly idiophones.

The *ipu heke* was originally constructed from gourds that long ago grew profusely in the Hawaiian islands and have just recently begun being cultivated there again. The *ipu heke 'ole* is constructed of a single large bottle gourd from which the top has been sliced. The *ipu heke* is a much larger instrument, constructed of two large gourds fastened together with strong glues. Sometimes a third gourd is used to make a collar to strengthen the join. A ribbon of cheesecloth impregnated with glue may also be used to reinforce the join. Both the *ipu heke 'ole* and *ipu heke* are held by a handle or cord wrapped around the narrow neck.

To play, the player kneels in front of a padded surface and drops the *ipu* to make a resounding tone. The player then lifts the gourd and strikes the lower portion with

Left to right:

Ipu heke 'ole Artwork by Lorna Blackburn

Ipu heke Courtesy of the Kauai Museum, Lihue, Hawaii

Ipu heke painted with heat Artwork and photo by B. Ka'imiloa Chrisman, M.D.

Ipu heke carved and painted Artwork by C. Siles Molina

the flat of the hand or with the fingers, thus creating a pulsing rhythm that inspires the hula dancers to more and more intense movements.

The *ipu heke 'ole* and *ipu heke* continue to be played by students of the hula, but they are no longer the exclusive domain of men. During the hula celebrations, additional music is supplied by the gourd rattles (*uli-uli*), singing, and clapping.

Shaken Instruments

Shakers

Gourds are probably most familiar as shakers and rattles used around the world. The distinction between "shaker" and "rattle" is primarily in the use of a handle and the way of playing. A shaker is a small container (the specific shape is relatively unimportant) that is cupped in the palm and shaken rhythmically. It can have a variety of noisemakers, each of which will produce a different sound. Today most shakers have small plastic beads or shot inside to produce a soft percussive sound.

Gourd palm rattles *Artwork by Ginger Summit*

Both ornamental gourds and small hardshell gourds make ideal containers for shakers. Drill a ⅜- to ½-inch hole in one end of a gourd, and clean out as much of the seeds and pulp as possible. Soak in water for a day to loosen stubborn pieces. A chopstick, bamboo skewer, or dental pick can help you reach around the interior. Then let the gourd dry completely. Coating the interior with varnish to seal the surface will increase the sound resonance. Add beads, seeds, or pebbles gradually, and test the sound by putting a finger over the hole while gently shaking. Experiment with different materials, such as rice, beans, corn, gravel, or small plastic beads, to find a sound that is pleasing. Plug the hole with a wood dowel plug (available in many sizes in hardware stores) or a cork, or glue on a piece of leather. If you use a removable plug, you can change the noisemakers when desired.

Gourd palm rattle with noisemaker material
Artwork by Ginger Summit

A simple shaker/rattle can be made by using the top of a bottle gourd by cleaning the cup and smoothing the bottom edge. Cut a circle disk from a scrap of gourd, leather, or wood to plug the opening. Add some noisemakers before gluing the disk on the cup. Use the stem of the gourd as a natural handle, or add a loop of leather to create a strap.

Rattles

Gourd rattles generally have a handle (which is either part of the natural gourd shape or is added on), and frequently have a brilliant percussive sound. Unlike today, when rattles are playthings for babies, rattles once were significant instruments to accompany song, dance, social and political ceremonies, and religious incantations. Specific rituals and taboos evolved to designate not only who could play a rattle, but under what circumstances, and who could make or even touch this sacred sound source.

Gourd rattles *Artwork by Dyan Petersen*

In many cultures throughout North and South America, Africa, India, and the Far East, rattles have been considered the sacred instrument of the tribal healer or shaman. Only that person was allowed to make or play the instrument, and the

Gourd rattle from Kenya

Pair of maracas from Costa Rica *From the collection of JoAnnis Mohrman*

rattle was the primary means of communication with the spirits or the ancestors. Often the instrument itself came to hold special magical powers. Various tribes in Africa, South America, and North America regard the rattle as either the dwelling place of the great spirits, the ancestor spirits, or even the devil.

In many Native American ceremonies, particularly in the Southwest, rattles are carried by the dancers to emphasize their movements, or are played by a chorus that accompanies the dancers. Historically, women and children were not allowed to touch the rattle, which was an integral part of the participants' costume and image.

Even today, among the Gourd Dancers of many Plains Indian tribes, great reverence and care surround the gourd rattle. No one except the owner/dancer is allowed to touch it, and during the dance ceremony its sounds are thought to communicate directly to the spirit world. It is only natural that an instrument integral to so many social activities would have many regulations regarding construction, decoration, and methods of use.

To increase the sound, noisemakers are commonly added, but the choice of noisemakers too has been long governed by tradition.

Simple—no handle added

The first rattle was probably a gourd that was picked up and shaken, with little or no change being made to this natural container. The narrow portion of a

Rattle

Materials	Tools
small dipper gourd	saw
paints, marking pens, dyes	scraper
	glue
noisemakers (pebbles, beads, seeds)	

Cut a wavy line in the gourd bowl where the gourd is at its widest diameter.

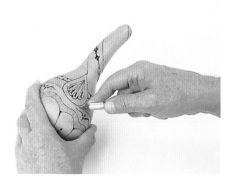

Scrape the inside of the gourd until it is clean. Paint the cut edge black with a marking pen.

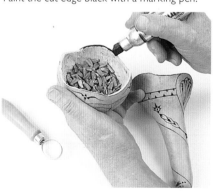

Put in the pebbles, shells, noisemakers, etc., and glue the two parts back together. *Artwork by Duane Teeter*

Gourd rattle with pyro-engraved, dyed sections of dipper gourd cut and tied to a handle
Artwork by Carolyn Rushton

Gourd rattle *Artwork by Nancy Schlender*

Pair of *hosho* rattles *Artwork by Mylinda King*

Pair of *hosho* rattles, from the Shona/Zezuru people of Zimbabwe. These gourds are planted among other crops for protection from the sun and are revealed at harvest time. Note the sewn patch over the entry hole.
Photo by fine arts students, Rhodes University
From the collection of the International Library of African Music, Rhodes University, Grahamstown, South Africa

dipper or bottle gourd suffices as the handle, the seeds act as the sound source, and the shell is either left plain or minimally decorated. A simple adaptation is to pierce the rattle with several small holes to allow more sound to emerge.

One example in which the gourd is only slightly modified is the *hosho* rattle. The *hosho*, played by the Shona in Zimbabwe to accompany the *mbira*, is made of the *maranka* (or dolphin gourd), which is a type of dipper gourd with a natural handle shape. To prepare the rattle, the insides are thoroughly cleaned through a small hole cut near the handle. The seeds are replaced with gravel, seeds, or even varnished popping corn. The hole is then sealed with a stopper or cork or sewn shut.

Similar simple gourd rattles have been used throughout North and South America and other parts of Africa. In Uganda, the opening is often closed with raffia basket coiling (similar to darning a sock!).

Handle added

More frequently handles have been attached to gourds of varying shapes and sizes. Many methods have been devised for this attachment.

Simple handle

The simplest is to make a hole in the side or end of the gourd, remove the contents, then insert a stick and secure the joint with sap, pitch, or glue. This creates a permanent seal, one that can be reinforced easily if it becomes loose after use. For a more secure join, the end of the handle can be carved so that the handle is wider than the narrow end, which is inserted into the gourd. This creates a shoulder for the gourd to rest on. The gourd is cleaned and filled with a sound source prior to inserting the handle.

Gourd rattles with stick handles *Left artwork by Orlando Hernandez, right artwork by Daniel Randolph*

African gourd rattle with bone handle. The handle is stitched in place. *From the collection of Ginger Summit*

Hopi Indian rattle from New Mexico *Artwork by Lyle Lomayam*

Gourd rattle with jawbone handle *Artwork by Natalie Sylvester*

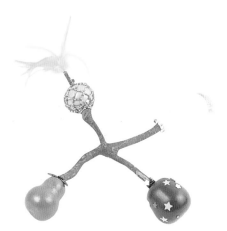

Double gourd rattle with wood handles *Artwork by Laura Nagle*

A familiar rattle that is made with this type of construction is the maraca, found in Mexico, the Caribbean, and South America. Maracas are usually played in pairs and are "tuned" so the two rattles play different frequencies. Not only are they often found as novelty or tourist items; maracas are a common accompaniment to dancing and singing, from traditional dances to informal street performances.

Gourds are not always attached to just a simple handle. In Cuba, rattles are used that have gourds attached to the four points of two crossed sticks.

Through-gourd handle

Materials

small gourd
small stick (½-inch diameter), for handle
noisemakers (pebbles, beads, seeds)
varnish, wax, dye

Tools

drill with ¼- and ⅜-inch drill bits
knife
file or rasp

Left: Carve the handle downward, so there is a shoulder for the gourd to rest against. Carve the handle to fit a ¼-inch hole. A ¼-inch drill bit is shown for comparison.

Below: Drill a small hole at the top.

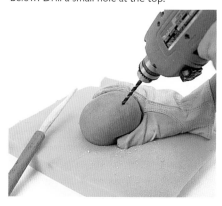

Various materials for noisemakers, including seeds and beads

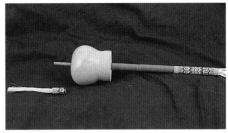

Above: Peyote rattle *Artwork by Michael Lopez*

Left: Gourd rattle of 24-inch length *Artwork by Lazaro Arvisu From the collection of Xavier Quijas Yxayotl*

A more secure handle construction involves making holes on both sides of a gourd so the narrow end of the handle can protrude out the opposite side. Holes are made on opposite sides of the gourd, one smaller than the other. The handle is carved to taper on the end, and is then inserted through the two holes in the gourd. A tiny hole is drilled through the narrow tip end of the handle, through which a small peg is pushed to secure the handle firmly in place. This innovation allows the handle to be removed and the noisemakers replaced, thus creating a "tunable" rattle. This particular design is found frequently in rattles from the American Southwest, and is especially identified with the peyote rattle used by the North American Church.

Gourd rattle *Artwork and photo by Susan Sweet*

Woven handle

Among the Polynesians, a woven innovation was used to create a handle.

First three or four holes were drilled in the gourd top, sufficiently large to clean out the seeds and pith. Then strips of *hau* fiber were pulled through the

Add materials to the gourd.

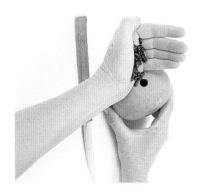

Insert the handle so the gourd rests against the shoulder. Drill a small hole in the narrow end of the handle at the top of the gourd.

Insert a dowel in the small hole, and trim.

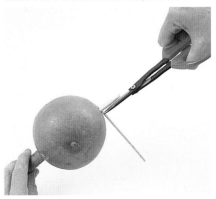

Uli'uli

Materials

small gourd

#4 basket reed
  weaving material,
  such as day-lily
  leaves, iris leaves,
  yarn

feathers

Tools

saw

drill with 3/16-inch
  drill bit

holes, and these were brought together and wrapped with *olona* cord to form a handle.

The *uli'uli* rattle became greatly embellished by the hula dancers in Hawaii. The ends of the *ie'ie* were woven enough to create a handle, and then were fanned out to form a disk that was covered with *tapa* cloth and elaborate feather designs. Unlike most other rattles, the *uli'uli* is held by the dancer with the feather disk facing upward and the gourd facing down. This rattle is so important that a dance is specifically named after it. The rattle is the only accompaniment for the dance, during which it is shaken and struck on the palm of the hand, on the thigh, and on the ground.

Dried day-lily leaves and canna lily seeds (*ali-ipoe*)

Basket reed is strung through four holes drilled into the top of a cleaned-out gourd.

The spokes are separated and twined together into a handle with the day-lily leaves. Twining consists of twisting two elements around each other while one of the elements passes in front of the warp and the other passes behind the warp. Then the positions are reversed.

The element on the left is brought in front of the first warp strand and then behind the second strand. Then the new element on the left repeats the same pattern. They twist around each other automatically with each stitch.

The weave continues. When the handle is the desired length, the warp strands are fanned out to form a flat disk and the weaving continues. Extra warp pieces will be added to keep the spacing between the warp strands consistent.

The finished *uli'uli* hula rattle *Artwork by Rebecca Lewis*

Ulili rattle (yo-yo rattle) made from three tree gourds *Artwork by Pohaku Nishimitsu.*

How to Play

Just as there are many different forms of gourd rattles, there are also many different ways to play them. The *uli'uli* is held with the gourd facing the ground, while most rattles are held upright directly in front of the musician or dancer. The Iroquois begin a song/dance with a high tremolo effect created by rapidly shaking the gourd rattle high in the air. As an accompaniment, the rattle is usually shaken in front of the chest, either with a forward fling of the arm, or a rhythmic side-to-side motion. Frequently, if the player is holding only one rattle, it is beaten or slapped against the other palm or the thigh. Among the Shona in Zimbabwe, the *hosho* is played with an up-and-down movement of the forearm to accompany the *mbira*.

Ulili

An unusual gourd rattle called the *ulili*, the *kani nui,* or the singing gourd rattle is found in Hawaii. It consists of three small round gourds on a single stick. The two outer gourds have seeds in them and are permanently mounted to the ends of the stick with glue or pitch. The smaller center gourd has large holes on either side of the center through which the stick turns easily. Midway between the two holes on the side of the center gourd is a third hole. A string that has been firmly attached to the center of the stick is brought out through this third hole. To play the rattle, hold the center gourd firmly and turn the stick so the string rolls up around it inside the center gourd. Pull the string rapidly, causing the outer two gourds to turn and rattle vigorously, and then immediately allow the string to slacken. It should roll back up on the stick (much as a yo-yo rewinds), so that to keep the rattle in motion the player needs only to pull the string. The stick will turn in the opposite direction with each pull.

Hawaiian girls playing the *uli'uli* *Photo by Kathy Long.*

A colorful group of *caxixi*

Caxixi (pronounced "ca-shi shi'")

Materials

gourd shell fragment, 4-inch diameter
#3 basket reed, five 36-inch lengths,
    for spokes
noisemakers (beads, seeds)

Tools

drinking cup, for template
saw
leather awl or ice pick

Another form of rattle uses a piece of gourd as the base of a small basket. This small shaker is rarely used by itself, but most often as an accessory to the *berimbau,* a musical bow, in Brazilian *capoeira.*

To play this instrument, the musician slips the *caxixi* over two or three fingers on the hand that taps the *berimbau* string with a stick. This creates an additional percussion sound and rhythm accompaniment to the *capoeira* music.

See page 72 for more discussion.

Far left: *Berimbau* with *caxixi* rattle *Artwork by Oscar Baeza*

Left: *Caxixi* *Artwork by Oscar Baeza*

Use a cup to draw a template for the bottom of the *caxixi* on a scrap piece of gourd. The bottom is about three to four inches across. The harder shell is to the inside.

Drill nine holes around the edge of the bottom using an awl or an ice pick. The holes should be just large enough to allow the reed to pass through. One hole must be slightly larger to accommodate two pieces of reed.

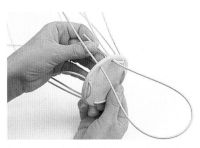

Loop a length of reed through two holes. Loop the next three through the two adjacent holes. The last loops through the one remaining hole and the adjacent hole that already has a strand in it. Treat these two strands as one.

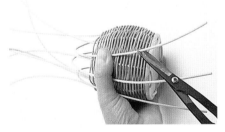

Weaving. Fold a 60-inch strand in half around one of the vertical spokes, so both halves of the strand point outward. Place the strand to the left in front of the first vertical spoke, then behind the next vertical spoke, and then out the next space between the two spokes.

Weaving. Now the second weaving element is on the left and repeats the previous step: in front of the first vertical spoke, behind the next vertical spoke, and out the next space.

When you run out of a weaver, add a new one by placing it behind the current vertical spoke and continuing with the weaving.

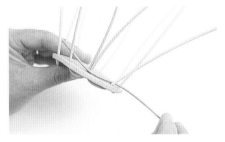

Cut the excess length from the spoke.

Use an ice pick to make room next to the spoke for the return spoke to slip in.

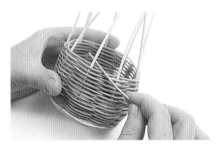

Insert noisemakers and continue weaving to seal the sound chamber.

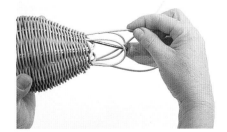

Insert the two spokes from one side along the spoke on the opposite side. Leave enough height for your hand to fit comfortably in the loop.

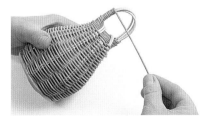

Wrap the handle with the balance of the weaver.

Insert the end of the wrapper into the weave to finish off. *Artwork by Chris Johnson*

29

Rain Stick

A rain stick is a unique form of rattle that was used by the Indians in Meso America during ceremonies at the time of spring planting. Two different shapes of rain stick were made to represent the male and female spirits. While other materials such as bamboo and hollowed stalks are more readily associated with rain sticks today, many shapes of gourds have been used for this instrument.

1. Select a snake or bottle gourd. Cut one end and thoroughly clean the interior. Once all the seeds and pulp are removed, the interior can be coated with varnish or sealer to create a more brilliant sound.
2. Knot four strings together and secure them at one end of the gourd. Wrap them in counterclockwise diagonal spirals around the gourd all the way to the base, and trace the lines with a pencil.
3. Using a leather awl, poke holes every 1–1½ inches along the diagonal lines.
4. Cut bamboo skewers or wooden dowels in lengths just over three-quarters of the diameter of the gourd. (You will want them to overlap inside the gourd but not touch each other or the opposite side of the shell.) Sharpen the ends of the dowels and insert into the holes, gluing in place. (Tapering the ends of the dowels will produce a melodious "ping" as the seeds hit the ends of the dowel.) After the glue is completely dry, sand the ends of the dowels so the exterior surface is completely smooth.
5. When the glue is dry, put noisemakers in the gourd. Test several different types of seeds, gravel, shot, or beads to find a pleasing effect.
6. Glue the gourd back together or attach a disk of leather over the opening.
7. Decorate.

Right: Rain stick

Below: Detail of the end of the rain stick. The end is sealed with another short tip of a dipper gourd. *Artwork by Carolyn Rushton*

Right: Invented and made by Xavier Quijas Yxayotl, the water gourd is made like a rain stick. This instrument is 30 inches long. It is played by holding rattan sticks in both hands and twisting and turning. It is filled with shells and little rocks. It sounds like ocean waves or a rippling brook. *Artwork by Xavier Quijas Yxayotl*

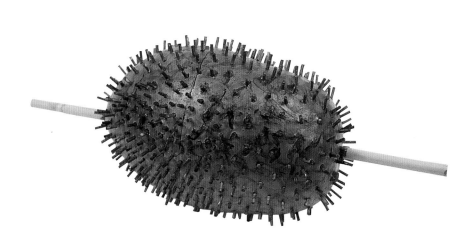

Cut open at one end and clean out the gourd.

Tie four strings together and tape them to the end of the gourd. Spiral the four strands down the body of the gourd, taping them in place.

Use a tin awl or an icepick to make holes along the marked spiral

Insert the skewer.

Before setting the skewer flush into the gourd, dab a little glue on the end of the skewer.

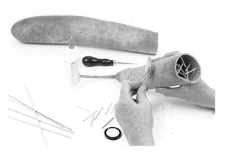

Use the bowl of a spoon to smooth the skewer flush with the gourd.

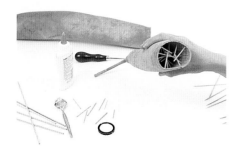

Detail of the inside of the rain stick, showing the skewer pattern

Various noisemakers that can be put inside the rain stick before the two parts are glued back together

Completed rain stick *Artwork by Ginger Summit*

Rain Stick

Materials

snake gourd

leather dye

noisemakers (pebbles, seeds, beads)

bamboo skewers

leather scrap

feathers

Tools

saw

scraper, to clean interior

leather awl or ice pick

glue

Shekere (pronounced "SHA-ku-re")

Materials

bottle gourd

80 ft #15 or
    #18 seine twine

250 pony beads
    (glass or plastic)

Tools

saw

scraper, to clean
    interior

short awl

tape

One of the most common forms of gourd rattle in Africa is the *shekere*. From there it was brought by slaves to the Western Hemisphere. It was then used in dances in South and Central America and the Caribbean, where it is still a very popular instrument.

Many other names are associated with *shekere: axatse* (Ghana), *agbe* (Nigeria), *lilolo* (Congo). The *agbe* is usually made of a very large gourd. It is also known

The end of nylon seine twine is melted to keep it from unraveling. The gourd is taped to a weighted container to maintain its position.

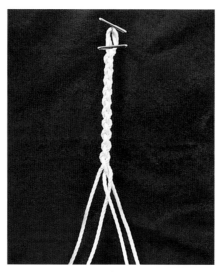

Fold two lengths of twine in half and weave a four-part braid long enough to go around the top of the gourd loosely.

Bring the loose ends of the braid through the loop at the top of the braid and tie a knot.

Fold a three-foot length of netting string in half and attach it by dropping the loose ends through the loop at the top. (This is the lark's-head knot.) Attach 25 lengths in this fashion, evenly spaced around the collar.

Cinch tight all the lark's-head knots, then tie an overhand knot to secure the knots. Taking one strand from one pair of strands and one strand from the adjacent pair of strands, tie an overhand knot, using the awl to place the knot exactly where you want it.

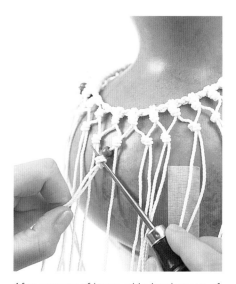

After one row of knots, add a bead on one of each pair of strands that you tie using adjacent strands from separate pairs of knots.

Detail of bead pattern

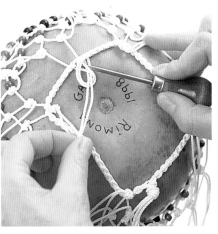

After completing the beading, make another four-part braid, tie it together, and anchor it to the bottom of the netting at four equal points.

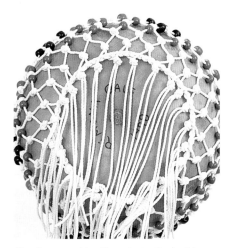

Continue attaching the pairs to the braid.

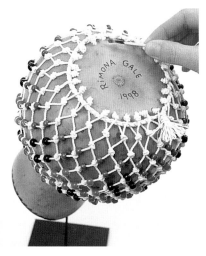

Trim the ends just short of the knot, then melt the ends to fuse them so they won't unravel.

The completed project *Artwork by Rimona Gale*

occasionally as *chocalcho, asson, achere,* and *cabaca. Shekere* is sometimes spelled *chekerie* or *sheKere.*

While there are several variations of *shekere,* all share an important common element: a gourd covered by a loose-fitting net, into which are woven hard objects. These vary depending on location and what is available: fish bones, glass beads, cowrie shells, seed pods, metal jangles, pieces of bamboo, or millet. The size of the gourd ranges from a small bottle gourd with a six-inch diameter of the larger bulb, to very large gourds with diameters up to 20 inches.

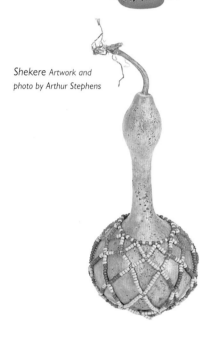

Shekere Artwork by Abdi Rashid Jibril.

Shekere Artwork and photo by Arthur Stephens

An opening of up to three inches is made in either the base of the gourd or in the stem end. The seeds and pulp are thoroughly removed, and sometimes the gourd is varnished or sealed with paint or sealer on the inside to create a more brilliant resonance.

Usually the netting is anchored on a string or ring of leather that rests loosely on the shoulder of the larger base, just below the neck of the bottle gourd. The soundmakers are added to the netting in a way that creates a decorative pattern and sometimes completely covers the bulb end of the gourd. The ends of the netting can be either tied with a single overhand knot at the base of the gourd or worked into a ring that becomes a temporary stand for the instrument when it is not being played. The netting can be very dense and close fitting or can be loosely woven. The variation depends on the musician, the custom within his community, and the style of music.

How to Play

Many different sounds can be produced by the *shekere* in the hands of a good musician. Initially, it is supported loosely by both hands, with the right hand cradling the neck of the gourd and the left hand supporting the base. Some of the different sound effects are created by:

1. tossing gently from hand to hand
2. shaking with one hand
3. tapping with fingers, the palm of one hand, or both hands
4. twisting the gourd within the netting

Shekeres usually accompany other instruments, especially the drum, and singing. They are often used by dancers and singers in ceremonies, parades, and public events.

A Brazilian variation of the *shekere* is called the *cabaza*. Typically smaller than

Shekere on lap is beaten with hands. Artwork by Eric Kelly

The tail is twisted to make the netting go around the gourd. *Artwork by Eric Kelly*

The gourd is supported at the neck with one hand, with the other hand tapping and tossing the gourd up and letting gravity pull it back down. Rapid finger tossing can set up syncopation. *Artwork by Eric Kelly*

the traditional *shekere,* it is made much like a rattle with a handle added. Around the outside of the gourd is a loose net of beads. Usually it is played by twisting the rattle, creating a swishing sound as the gourd scrapes against the beaded net. Modern adaptations called *afuches* are found in contemporary percussion collections where the gourd is replaced by a dimpled metal sphere, and the covering is a network of metal beads.

Above: The *shekere* can also be played by being tossed and spun. *Artwork by Daniel Randolph*

Left: The *shekere* is held in one hand. The other hand slaps the netting upward to make it spin around the gourd. *Artwork by Daniel Randolph*

Knocked Together

Sistrum

A *sistrum* is an idiophone that relies on two or more objects clapping together to make noise. It has many forms, and has been used as a percussion instrument throughout the world; even today it is often a part of celebrations and religious festivals, particularly in the Middle East. One common form consists of an open Y-shaped frame with wires stretched between two upright sides. Disks of metal or wood are strung along the wires, which make a sound when shaken. While most styles of *sistrum* played today are made of wood and metal, in sub-Saharan Africa gourds are used for all or part of the instrument.

Frequently disks made of gourds are used in place of the metal disks. This creates a very different sound—one that is usually softer or more muffled than the traditional metal disks.

A related form uses the gourd as the framework. Two sides are cut off the bulb of a bottle gourd or short-handled dipper gourd, thus creating a hollow circular frame with a handle attached. Metal wires are stretched across the opening, and metal or gourd disks are strung on each. The gourd acts as a resonator, amplifying the sounds of the disks.

Shekere rattles *Artwork and photo by Lupe Molina*

Sistrum from Kenya

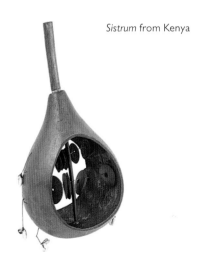

35

Kenyan
sistrum

Sistrum Artwork
by Dyan Peterson

Sistrum Artwork
by Pat Wilkinson

Kenyan
lala

The Kenyan *lala* is played by rapidly raising
and lowering the handles, making the disks fall
on top of each other. *Artwork by Daniel Randolph*

Stick Clapper, or *Lala*

The stick clapper is a common idiophone in the West African countries of Mali,
Burkina Faso, and Guinea. It has gourd disks strung on one end of a bent
branch. The disks are held in place by a stopper, or, in rare cases, by decorated
netting. When played, the disks make a loud clapping sound. It is traditionally
played in rituals connected to the life cycle. In Gambia such disk rattles are
known as *lala*.

Tambourine

A tambourine-like instrument is made of many shells, seedpods, or beads thread-
ed around the outer periphery of a gourd bowl. Lengths of seeds are also strung
and hang down or knock against the gourd shell. It can be played by shaking the
bowl or by slapping it with the opposite hand, jarring the beaded decorations
against the shell.

Left: Pieces from the neck of the dipper
gourd are attached around this gourd mask as
noisemakers. *Artwork by Carolyn Rushton*

Below: African tambourine *From the collection of
Ethnic Arts, Berkeley, California*

Tambourine *Artwork by Honeybear Miller*

Above: African rasp *From the collection of Virginia Umberger*

Left: Hemis mana painting by Sher Lynn Elliot-Widess

Scraped

Rasp

A rasp consists of a rough surface against which another object is rubbed or scraped. In its simplest form, a notched stick is rubbed with a smooth stick or bone in a rhythmic pattern.

To enhance the sound produced, the object with the notches is combined with a resonator, usually a gourd but sometimes a basket. The slow rubbing of the rasp used in the *Kachina* dances of the American Southwest Pueblo Indians imitates the grinding of the corn on metates. The notched stick is placed over a gourd bowl resonator and then scraped with a sheep scapula to create the sound. Variations of this are also found in northern Mexico as well as Africa.

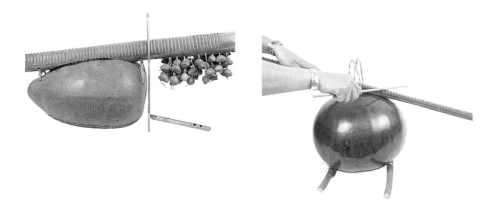

Left: Rasp *Artwork by Xavier Quijas Yxayotl*

Far left: The Aztec name for this rasp is *omichicahuastl*. It is played by rubbing a bamboo stick across the notched stick. The pods that hang from the rasp are also fondled while playing to elicit another sound. Often the rasp player will play a flute with one hand while he plays the rasp with his other hand. *Artwork by Xavier Quijas Yxayotl*

Guiro

Materials

snake gourd

varnish

chopstick

Tools

saw

drill

riffler rasp

scraper, to clean interior

small torch, to decorate instrument (optional)

Guiro Artwork by Duane Teeter

The more familiar form of rasp, or *guiro,* has the notches carved on the side of the hollow resonator. This is still found throughout the Caribbean, Mexico, and Central and South America. (In Cuba it is known as a *raspa.*) Usually two or more holes are made in the shell, both to allow thorough cleaning of the pulp and seeds and to provide finger holes to hold the instrument. The shape and size of the resonator can vary, and today artists are creating unusual and beautiful instruments that are works of art as well as objects to be played.

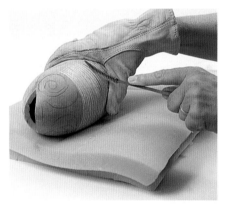

Use a riffler rasp to cut grooves into the side of the cleaned-out gourd.

Drill two finger/sound holes in the bottom of the gourd.

Use a small butane torch to decorate the *guiro.* Artwork by Ginger Summit

Guiro Artwork by Ginger Summit

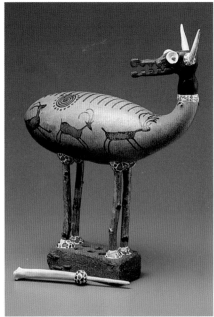

Above left: *Guiro, "The Gathering"* Artwork by
Burnt Offerings Studio, Opie and Linda O'Brien Photo by
Opie O'Brien

Above right: *Guiro, "Xibalba"* Artwork by Burnt
Offerings Studio, Opie and Linda O'Brien Photo by Opie
O'Brien

Lamellaphones

Lamellaphones produce sounds by plucked lamella, or tines, which are securely fastened to a base. Historically the tines have been made of wood or bamboo, but today most are made of metal, which can be easily shaped and tuned, and which produces a good vibration when plucked or struck. Usually the sound produced this way is soft, so the baseboard holding the lamella is attached in some way to a resonating container or vessel to enhance the sound.

Music Box

A familiar instrument that illustrates the principles of the lamellaphone is the music box. The sound-producing mechanism for this instrument consists of a rotating drum with pegs and a metal piece with tiny metal tongues (resembling a comb) that is firmly secured next to the drum. To play, a key winds a spring, which in turn causes the drum to rotate slowly. Pegs on the drum selectively pluck the tiny metal keys to produce a melody. Standing alone, this mechanism produces little sound, so it is almost always attached to the top or inside of a box or resonator, which amplifies the sounds produced.

Music box inside a gourd *Artwork by Ginger Summit*

Mbira

The *mbira* is a family of instruments that is indisputably African in origin. It is found in almost all cultures throughout sub-Saharan Africa, and in a wide variety of forms, shapes, and sizes. It was brought by slaves to the Western Hemisphere, where it is now a popular folk instrument, especially in the Caribbean and in the southeastern

Washboard breastplate, to be worn on the chest and rubbed with gourd thimbles on fingertips and/or gourd sticks *Artwork by Minnie Black*

United States. Because the instrument has been used over the centuries by so many different tribes and cultures, it has acquired many different names. Here we will use the term "*mbira*" to refer to the instruments that are generally used in Africa, and "*kalimba*" to those that are European influenced and are more frequently seen in the United States.

The Grove Dictionary of Musical Instruments lists over 190 names, because this is actually a large category of related instruments. There are three distinct forms of *mbira*-type instruments, each of which is favored in different parts of Africa and elsewhere around the world.

The features that are common to all three forms are: a keyboard consisting of several lamella mounted on a body that radiates sound, a resonator, and a soundboard, which may or may not be permanently attached to the resonator.

The number of lamella, or tines, varies dramatically from three to 40. Originally the lamella were made of strips of bamboo, bark of raffia palm, rattan cane, or other similar resilient material. Today wood has been largely replaced by metal, although large wooden keys are occasionally seen in the *basse en boîte* (bass box or rumba box), a large instrument played in Jamaica and Cuba.

While the wood base to which the lamella are fastened greatly affects the sound, no single wood is specified for that purpose, although a hardwood is definitely preferred.

Buzzers are considered an important component of the *mbira* sound, so objects are often attached to the lamella. Small metal collars, beads, or rings are strung directly onto the tines at the bridge. Trade beads or metal pieces are occasionally fastened to the soundboard itself.

The methods by which lamella are attached to the soundboard are as varied

Playing the *mbira* *Photo by William Simpson*

as the cultures throughout Africa. Some are assembled in haste, while others are created with great care and experience. Simple *mbira* of three to eight lamella, found in West Africa, are usually made and played by individuals for their own enjoyment and at casual gatherings. Other instruments with 30 or more lamella are constructed and are often stacked in up to three tiers. The more elaborate forms with larger keyboards and more complex musical traditions are found in Zimbabwe or southern Africa.

Because the lamella on a baseboard alone do not produce much sound, this framework is usually combined in some way with a resonator:

- The keyboard is simply rested on top of a small, open gourd, which may or may not have a hole in the side. Occasionally a ceramic or plastic pot is substituted for the gourd.
- The second method consists of a single soundboard placed inside a large resonating chamber, called the *deze,* traditionally a large gourd. This form of *mbira* is most often found in southern Africa, where the *mbira* is considered a national instrument of Zimbabwe.

The keyboard is wedged securely within the resonator with a stick, in direct contact with the resonating chamber in several places. The musician can play the instrument with the resonator resting on his lap or on a surface in front of him. Because the soundboard is wedged securely, he can also hold the instrument while standing and walking.

Other important components of the resonating gourd are buzzers, which are frequently attached around the outer periphery. Originally these were pieces of shell, but in modern times these have been replaced by bottle caps or other pieces of metal. Their purpose is to prolong the sounds; the *mbira* sound is not considered emotionally satisfying without them. However, there is a great difference between the sounds created by the shells and those produced by bottle caps. The choice depends on the musician and the musical community.

While originally the resonating container was a large gourd, in recent times it is occasionally replaced by a large plastic or fiberglass bowl. The sounds that each of these containers resonates can be quite different.

- The form of *mbira* still frequently seen in West Africa and most prevalent in America today consists of the soundboard permanently attached to a resonator, either a half-gourd or a wooden box. Occasionally a tin can or even a tortoise shell is used.

Often the box or gourd has one or two holes in the side, which the player covers with his fingers to modulate the sound. In the United States this instrument is commonly called a thumb piano or *kalimba.*

MBIRA

The *mbira* is a family of instruments. Some of its members are:

kalimba or *marimba*	Zaire
mbira	Zimbabwe, southern Africa
njari	southern Zimbabwe
sanza	Bantu
zanza	equatorial Africa
kembe	Central African Republic
lukembe, likembe	Congo and Zaire
agidibo	Nigeria
gibinji	Congo
timbil	Cameroon
deze	Transvaal, South Africa
kankobele	Zambia
kone	Upper Volta
basse en boîte	Jamaica
thumb piano	United States

Other names are:

mbira huru	*bamboli*
abuboyo	*kasayi*
pokido	*Bashi*
malimbambira	*kaffir piano*
ambira	*biti*
zimba	*rumba box*
kalimba mbira	*madumba*

and this list is not complete!

Kalimba

Materials

medium gourd 8–10-inch diameter
¼-inch plywood 12 x 12 inches
1 x 4-inch hardwood block
U-shaped shelf wall bracket, for the bridge
three 2-inch machine screws and nuts
old metal leaf rake
varnish

Tools

saw
sandpaper
drill
pen and ruler
tin snips
glue
brush

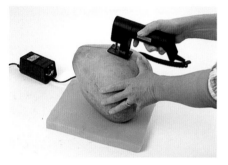

Cut the gourd in half.

Sand the cut edge until the entire cut is perfectly plane.

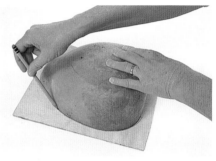

Mark the profile on thin plywood or board. Make sure that the final top side of the board is down.

Cut out the profile with a very fine toothed saw blade.

Mark the length on a hardwood block rod and a piece of cabinet shelf support for the bridge.

Cut the pieces to length for the bridge.

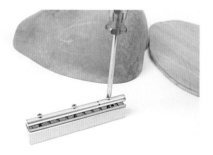

Assemble the bridge.

Left: Drill three holes in the bridge pieces.

Place the bridge on top and determine where the sound hole should be.

Cut the sound hole.

Glue the top to the gourd.

Use rubber bands to secure the top to the gourd while the glue dries.

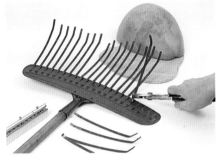

Cut keys (lamella) from an old leaf rake.

Position the keys in the bridge and tighten the screws. If you need to adjust the length of a key slightly, loosen the screw, then readjust it.

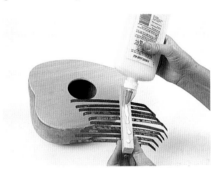

Glue the bridge to the top.

Tuning the *mbira*

Although there are many different ways to tune the *mbira,* they can be divided into two main traditions. The one that is most frequently found in America, and was undoubtedly influenced by the European musical tradition, uses eight or 12 keys graduated out from the center, with the longest (lowest) keys in the center, going up the scale alternately to the left and right of the center key. Occasionally a lower drone key is placed on the extreme right edge. The keys of many of the *mbira* found in West Africa are also arranged in this configuration.

The *mbira* made and played in southern Africa is usually constructed with a much different arrangement of keys. The keys are frequently grouped according to registers, so one hand plays the melody on the keys on the right side of the soundboard and the other plays the accompaniment or rhythm on the keys on the left.

Different cultures in Africa use the *mbira* for different functions, and each has special methods of construction and tuning. The number and organization of keys is one obvious distinguishing feature. Typically the keys range in number from five to 20, but some southern and East African instruments have as many as 45. The arrangement of keys is also an important distinction. In some tribes, the keyboard is described as a family group, with groups of keys representing the old men's, women's, or children's voices. The combined voices of all the keys thus

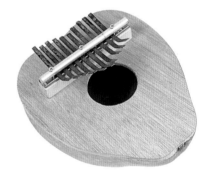

Completed kalimba *Artwork by Jim Widess and Ginger Summit*

Three African *mbira*

Hacksaw blades used for keys *Artwork and photo by Arthur Stephens*

Mbira *Artwork by Minnie Black*

Right: *Mbira* *Artwork by Glenda Allison*

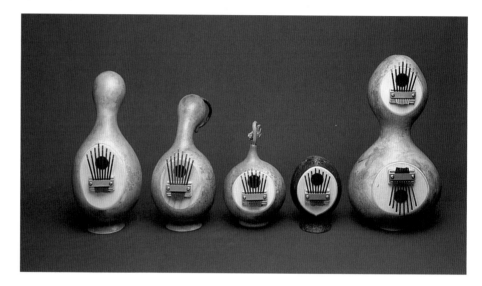

Madebe dza mhondoro mbira in its *deze* calabash resonator. Shona/Budya people, Northeast Zimbabwe. The land snail shell adds a buzz to the sound. The diameter of the calabash is 16.5 inches. *Photo by fine arts students, Rhodes University. From the collection of the International Library of African Music, Rhodes University, Grahamstown, South Africa*

embody the harmony within the family, the bringing together of the family members into a single unit.

Playing the *mbira*

The *mbira* is usually held with the sound box in the palms of the hands, leaving the thumbs free to pluck the tines and the index fingers to tap a rhythm on the resonator or modify the sound by stopping the holes in the resonator shell. Occasionally the index fingers pluck up on some of the outer tines. The idea of "right" or "wrong" melodic notes, so fundamental to Western ears, is of secondary importance in African music, where the principal concern is maintaining the rhythmic pulse without pause or break.

Hit (Complex)

Another idiophone that is used to play complex melodic music is the xylophone or marimba. While today metal or plastic pipes, wood boxes, or bamboo tubes are commonly used for resonators, traditional xylophones have gourds suspended

SOCIAL SIGNIFICANCE OF THE *MBIRA*

While it may not be readily apparent to an unsophisticated listener, different tunings are very distinct between individual tribes in Africa. Within a tribe or culture, the *mbira* will communicate sounds very closely related to the language, expressing deep sentiments about religion, ceremonies, family, and friends. Members of other groups may be unfamiliar with the tuning of the instrument as well as the method of playing, making the instrument's music difficult to recognize.

In central east and southeast regions of Africa the *mbira* is more often associated with religious and ritual contexts. In Zimbabwe, there are two forms of *mbira* that differ in form, tuning, and use. One form may be used by anyone for recreation and entertainment. Other forms, called *mbira dza vadzimu,* are used only in ancestral rituals and ceremonial performances. The right to own these *mbira* can be the exclusive right of chiefs, doctors and diviners, or shamans.

What may appear to be a simple instrument actually requires great effort and skill to master. Paul Berliner describes learning to play the *mbira* among the Shona in Zimbabwe as an endeavor that has taken many years. These people believe the skills develop only through the assistance of ancestors who appear in dreams, and that outsiders may develop the skills, but will never be truly great players without the blessing and assistance of the ancestors.

Like many other instruments, the voice of the *mbira* is frequently associated with complex social and religious meanings.

It may be played in social and political ceremonies in praise of chiefs or other important members of the community. Certain tunings and songs are associated with specific rituals, such as songs and dances that accompany initiation rituals or hunting celebrations.

Among the Shona (Zimbabwe) and the Bantu (Transvaal) the *mbira* is directly linked to the ancestral spirits. By playing the *mbira* at certain ritual gatherings (*bira*) it is possible to contact the ancestor spirits directly. Their presence either contributes to altered states or possession by the shaman, or allows the ancestors to be reincarnated into the bodies of other people present, to participate in dances.

The *mbira* was undoubtedly brought to the Western Hemisphere by the slaves from West Africa. It has been a very popular instrument throughout South America, the Caribbean, and the American Southeast. The forms of this instrument in this hemisphere reflect many of the varying styles in Africa. In South America, the style that used a soundbox inside a large gourd resonator was popular in the 19th century, but now is largely unknown. In the Caribbean, a small instrument that uses a box resonator attached to the soundboard is popular. Among the Afro-Cubans is a similar instrument nearly the size of a small suitcase, with from three to 10 steel tongues. Frequently called a *marimbula* or rumba box, this instrument provides a rhythmic and harmonic bass in folk and popular music groups.

Among the settlers in the American Southeast, the instrument was adapted to play familiar folk songs, either solo or along with other instruments. The American thumb piano usually has from eight to 12 keys and is tuned either to a diatonic or pentatonic scale. The arrangement of the keys is V-shaped, with the longest key (lowest note) in the center and the notes arranged alternately on either side. The keyboard is fastened securely either to a gourd or box resonator.

Mbira Artwork by Dan Tribe. From the Ethnic Arts Collection, Berkeley, California

Mhlahlazi Sithole plays his *mbira* at a spirit ceremony in Zimbabwe. *Photo by Andrew Tracey*

Guatemala marimba. Note the similarity to the African example on page 48. *Photo © 1998, Hector A. Menendez, Guatemala City, Guatemala*

West African *ilimba* Photo by Phyllis Ruttner

under the keys. Because each key has its own resonator, the superior skill of the xylophone maker is required in picking gourds and finessing them so they have the exact resonance of each key.

A form of xylophone may have been introduced to Africa from Southeast Asia around the first century. Early Indonesian xylophones used bamboo tubes for resonators, while African adaptations most frequently have gourds. *Bala* is the generic name for xylophone in Mali and Guinea. *Balafon* is the European term, which has been adapted from *bala* + *fon* (meaning "to speak"). Therefore *balafon* means "to play the *bala*."

Slaves from West Africa introduced several different forms to the Western Hemisphere. The style still made and played in Guatemala originally had gourds as resonators. These have largely been replaced by long, hexagonal wooden boxes that resemble their gourd ancestors. The Guatemalan xylophone is called a marimba.

Ilimba (Percussion Bar)

The simplest form of the xylophone is found in Zambia, where it is known as a percussion bar, and in Zimbabwe, where it is known as an *ilimba*. This instrument consists of a single wooden bar suspended over a slot or hole in a large gourd, suspended between two curved supports. The vibrations of the stricken bar are amplified by the hollow gourd.

This instrument provides a very good introduction to the relationship between the vibrations of a solid object, i.e., the wooden key and the resonator.

A freely suspended key will have a natural vibration throughout its body, which is maximum at the center. The nodes are points at which the object does not vibrate. If you hold the key at any other point your finger will damp some of the vibration. You can test this by holding the key or a stick of wood between your thumb and forefinger and hitting it gently with a mallet. Hold the wood at different points until the maximum tone is produced when the key is hit in its center. That point you are holding then is the node. There are two nodal points on each key, approximately one quarter the distance in from either end. These are the points on which they should be held or suspended by the instrument frame for maximum vibration in the center of the key.

Pieces of wood with different densities will have different vibration patterns and slightly different pitches. Explore this by testing several different keys, or pieces of wood of different lengths and thicknesses. There are two general principles: 1) The longer the piece of wood, the lower the tone, and 2) the thinner the wood, the lower the tone. These principles apply as long as you are comparing keys made from the same type of wood. Keep in mind, however, that density also affects the tone that is produced. The note can be adjusted by removing wood from the middle of the key to lower the note (making it relatively thinner at the maximum vibration point) or from the ends to raise it (effectively shortening the key).

Some keys sound much more vibrant than others when they are suspended over a gourd resonator. Just as the key has a natural frequency at which it vibrates, so does the enclosed air in the gourd resonator. The larger, or longer, the column of enclosed air, the lower the natural resonance. When the column of air has approximately the same natural pitch as the key held above it, they are "in resonance," and the sound will be greatly enhanced. If they have different natural pitches, the column of air will not make much difference and the bar will sound dull when tapped. You can make a temporary adjustment in the volume of the gourd resonator by pouring sand into the opening. Make permanent changes by enlarging the opening or cutting off part of the gourd. Many *ilimba* and *balafon* gourd resonators have holes in the side, which may or may not be covered with a thin membrane (a *miriliton*). This will also affect the resonating characteristics of the container, either raising or lowering the tone, depending on the tension of the membrane, as well as adding a buzzing sound.

Holding a key at the node and tapping the center to hear the key *Artwork by Ginger Summit*

Carving out the center of the key with a rasp to lower the tone *Artwork by Ginger Summit*

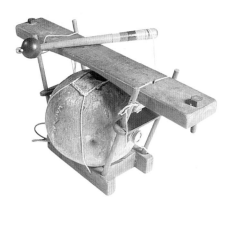

Left: The *ilimba* one-note xylophone the Nsenga people of Zambia use to accompany party songs. While striking the key with the right hand, the left is inserted between the key and the resonator. This alternately opens and closes the aperture, thereby creating different resonance effects. The diameter of the calabash is 6.75 inches. *Photo by fine arts students, Rhodes University From the collection of the International Library of African Music, Rhodes University, Grahamstown, South Africa*

Right: A modern *ilimba* made for "Wait a Minim," a stage show that played on three continents in the 1960s. The length of the key is 24.5 inches. *Photo by fine arts students, Rhodes University From the collection of the International Library of African Music, Rhodes University, Grahamstown, South Africa*

Xylophones

Many variations of xylophone are popular throughout Africa. Some consist of bars lined up over logs, straw bundles, or even the player's legs. These variations usually do not have additional resonators, unless the bars are lined up over a pit or a hole dug in the ground.

The xylophone gradually evolved from this primitive and temporary construction into many related but differing forms, assuming specialized roles according to the different cultures where it is used. The features common to all xylophones are a graduated series of wooden keys beneath which are suspended gourds to resonate the tones.

The wood used for the keys varies according to the location, but hardwood such as mahogany is most prized. Once a tree has been felled and the wood properly aged, individual keys are cut according to conventions of the individual communities. They can be pitched differently: both the Manding and Chopi tribes have large xylophone orchestras made up of soprano, alto, mezzo-soprano, bass, and contrabass instruments.

Most xylophones are long and permanently secured to a rigid frame. Some frames, however, are flexible and can be worn by a special harness around the neck and back, or can be braced in a tree or between sturdy supports. Xylophones can be played solo with one to three players performing on the instrument together, but usually they are played with other instruments. The beaters tend to be heavy, tipped with rubber from old tires. Usually two beaters are held in each hand, between the first and second fingers, in a manner that takes advantage of the leverage of the full forearm. Improvisation and virtuosity are important ways players may be distinguished, and there is a great deal of variation both in music and among players throughout the tribes in Africa.

As with other instruments that are used in many different tribal cultures,

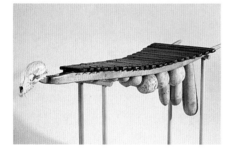

Top: ZeBear marimba, of zebrawood, gourd, wood, and bear skull *Artwork by Bill and Mary Buchen   Photo by Robert Nash*

Right: Zambian xylophones *Photo by Beany Wezelman*

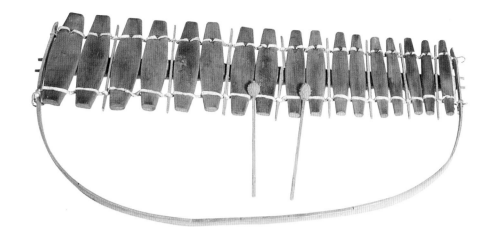

Muhambi xylophone of the Tswa people of southern Mozambique. Sneezewood keys resonated with matamba tree gourds and played in trios with drums for dancing. The xylophone is 45.5 inches inches.

Photo by fine arts students, Rhodes University. From the collection of the International Library of African Music, Rhodes University, Grahamstown, South Africa

specific rituals have evolved that prescribe who can play the instrument and when it can be played. In the Kilaya tribe in Nigeria, only one family is allowed to make, own, and play the small xylophones. In many other tribes, specialization in playing the instrument also tends to run in families, and children are encouraged to start early to learn playing techniques. Other members of the community may study or apprentice with a master if they show exceptional interest and talent.

In northwestern Ghana, societies are identified and tend to group themselves on the basis of how they tune xylophones, rather than according to language or other social factors. In Ghana, it is also a tradition that only men may play the instrument. A superstition persists that if a woman were to play one, she would be unable to bear children. While in some areas the instrument is considered sacred or the exclusive domain of selected families or cults, in most parts of Africa the xylophone is played for almost all musical occasions.

There are many contemporary music groups that play the xylophone today. This instrument and the *mbira* have become particularly popular through exposure on the radio and other public media, reawakening people to their cultural heritage. Popular musicians combine the xylophone with many other instruments to create a completely new musical sound. They have also been very successful in sharing this music with audiences around the world. Xylophone musicians often replace the gourd resonators with other, more durable materials, such as PVC pipe or wooden boxes, particularly when they are on tour. Students in areas where gourds are not available simply use materials at hand to create their own similar instruments. While the instruments often do not sound the same, the interest in the musical traditions is shared and enjoyed.

Part 2

Membranophones

The large category of membranophones includes most drums found in virtually all cultures worldwide. Unlike the idiophone drum, all other drums are constructed using a membrane that covers one or more openings in a hollow body. Striking causes a vibration in the membrane that is transmitted to the surrounding air. The body of the drum, and the enclosed air, resonate and further amplify the vibration. These two elements have been combined in many imaginative ways to create and amplify sounds.

The rigid frame of membranophones has been made of a wide variety of material. Musicians continue to experiment with new materials and shapes, for both the membrane and the body.

The frame can be as simple as a ring, but more frequently the bodies are made of wood, gourd, and, in recent times, plastics and metal. Drum bodies made of gourds are common where sturdy gourds are plentiful and logs with large diameters are not available, such as in the West African savannah, where the greatest variety of drums made with gourds (or calabash) are found. Most drums made of gourds are single-headed, although double-headed gourd drums are becoming more common.

The choice of material for the drum head can vary greatly. Usually it is the skin of a local animal, such as a goat, sheep, cow, or antelope. In Central America, drum membranes have been made of monkey skin, snake, and lizard; and in the Arctic, Eskimos have used seal bladder for membranes.

In northwestern Ghana, large drums made with two pitches are played exclusively by men at important ceremonies, particularly political events. The Ashanti make a similar drum called the *pintim* or *mpintimtoa,* which is played specifically to announce the arrival of an important person to the community. A

Top: A large kettle-type drum is found in Burkina Faso, Mali, and northern Ghana, where it is known as a *binha, binder,* or *pentre.* Made from a single, very large, round gourd, the body of the drum is usually a diameter of 18 inches or more. The top of the gourd is sliced off and covered with goat hide. *From the collection of Ginger Summit*

Right: A gourd drum, the *dimdekim,* found in Nigeria, uses two large gourds fastened together with rope and dung, and is topped with a hollow wooden cylinder. *Photo by Marla C. Berns*

very similar instrument identified as a barrel drum is found in Madras, India. As in Africa, it is slung around the neck and played with both hands.

A gourd drum, the *dimdekim,* found in Nigeria, uses two large gourds fastened together with rope and dung, and topped by a hollow wood cylinder. It is played by the Yungur tribe only at funerals, since it is thought to be related directly to powerful ancestral forces, and when played establishes a connection with the spirits.

Drums constructed of smaller gourds are used by several tribes in northern Nigeria, including the Yoruba. These drums can be tuned to very specific pitches and are frequently used to communicate over distances, much like the well-known hourglass-shaped talking drum. A small hole is made in the lower portion of the gourd. One hand beats on the membrane cover, and the other opens or closes off part of the hole, thereby changing the pitch slightly.

Small gourd drums in North America were described by an architect named Latribe, who visited New Orleans in 1819. Based on his description of the instruments and the ways they were being played, it was clear they were very similar to instruments in Africa that are played even today.

Making a Drum

General Principles

There are three important elements in drum construction that greatly affect the sound of the instrument—the material used for the drum head, the attachment of the membrane to the frame, and the shape of the resonator.

Materials for a drum head

The classification for drums is called membranophones for good reason—the traditional material for creating the initial vibration is a stretched membrane. The choice of membrane is extremely wide and has mostly been influenced by what is immediately available to the instrument maker. Rawhide skins of almost all animals have been used, but cow skin (for especially large drums) and goat skin are most common. Drum heads of cat, pig, deer, rabbit, snake, lizard, and even monkey skin are not unusual. Untanned or raw animal skins that have been stretched and dried can be purchased from specialty leather stores. Rawhide is hard to work with and must be soaked in tepid water to soften. It can then be cut, stitched, rolled, or shaped to make a suitable head.

Drum heads can also be purchased from an instrument supplier, already cut and either attached to a hoop or prepared for mounting on a frame.

Other materials suitable for drum heads include a range of synthetic materials, films, and plastics. They can be purchased from music supply stores in a variety of weights and sizes. If you need only a small drum head, inquire about damaged heads. These are sometimes saved by music stores when they replace drum heads for customers. These can be trimmed to size and used once again.

Attachment of the drum head

The stretched membrane has a natural frequency at which it vibrates. To produce a rich sound, the natural resonance of the air cavity must be in the same general frequency range that allows it to reinforce the natural frequencies of the membrane. Because the drum head is an integral part of the wall of the drum body chamber, the two elements must be worked together to establish the optimum drum "voice." This is a process of adjustment of the tension of the head as well as the opening in the body to create the right balance between fundamentals and resonances.

The method of attachment of the drum head to the body is directly related to this issue. In many styles of drum, the tension of the stretched membrane can be adjusted to get an optimal balance. But the tension of the stretched membrane can be affected in many other ways as well. Weather is one factor that can have a dramatic effect. Dampness and humidity will cause a membrane to soften, while warm temperatures and dry air tend to make it rigid. If the drum head is permanently attached to a drum body, there are only a few ways these effects can be modified. Water can be sprinkled on the membrane, or a hair dryer can be used to dry it or warm it to affect the vibration pattern. In some drums in India, the player applies a dab of wheat paste to the center of the drum head just before performing to help achieve the right balance. (This is a temporary adjustment, not to be confused with the more permanent circle of iron paste in the center of *tabla* drums.)

Drum body shapes

The air chamber of the drum body greatly influences the sounds of the struck membrane by reinforcing different overtones. The deeper the chamber, the greater

Copy of *punio* made from a gourd, *kala* skin (unicorn fish), *ie'ie* roots tied in a hoop, then wrapped with tapa (bark cloth). It is tied with *olana* cord. The *ka'* (beater) is made of coconut cordage folded and knotted. The *kilu* (gourd) or *puniu* (coconut) could be worn on the knee of the drummer with leg ties or set on a cordage stand, as this one is. *Artwork by B. Ka'imiloa Chrisman, M.D.*

the resonance. The chamber can be open or closed, which affects the movement of the vibrating air within it as well as transmission of sounds to the listener. In a small closed chamber, vibrating air may actually dampen the vibrations of the membrane, thus producing a dull tone. The actual size of the opening in the chamber affects the overtones resonated, so experiment by gradually increasing the opening once the drum head is secure. Small single-headed drums usually are left open at the far end. Kettle drums, which have a large cavity within the bushel gourd body, generally do not need an additional opening to produce a rich sound.

Double-headed drums entirely enclose the air chamber, but the flexibility of the second head gives the enclosed air necessary freedom of movement. A hole in the side of a double-headed drum is often made to allow some air flow and therefore greater sound transmission.

Making a Drum—Step-by-Step Instructions

Materials	Tools
gourd—6–10-inch diameter	saw
rawhide skin—8–12-inch diameter	file
(enough to leave two inches around the	sandpaper
circumference of the gourd opening)	staples or tacks
decorative strip—48 inches	hammer
white glue	

When making a drum from a gourd, select any size and shape gourd with a sturdy thick shell and uniform circular diameter. An irregularly shaped gourd can be used, but it is more difficult to create and maintain even tension on the drum head.

1. Slice off the top of the gourd as evenly as possible. This can be done quite easily with a band saw, but with care a handsaw works just as well.
2. After you cut the gourd open, file and sand the cut edge until the surface is completely flat. Test by turning the gourd upside down on a flat surface. If you put a thin layer of chalk dust or flour on the surface of the table, you can tell which parts of the gourd shell are uneven. Sand the higher portions until the entire surface of the opening picks up the chalk dust evenly. For a smooth and tight fit of the membrane, you must eliminate any irregular or bumpy edges.

   In addition to being completely flat, the edge surface of the rim should be perfectly level. If it slopes to the inside, there will be a tendency for buzzes or rattles. The outer edge should be slightly rounded to allow for smoother conformity of the membrane to the gourd.

   If necessary, a reinforcement ring made of a thin strip of veneer or reed can be glued to the inside rim of the cut surface of a thin gourd shell. This will provide a support for staples or tacks used to secure a permanent drum head.
3. Cut a circle of the membrane that you have chosen that extends at least two inches beyond the edge of the opening. Soak the membrane in tepid water

Gourd drum *Artwork by Darrel Devore*

Cut off the end of a gourd.

Rasp the rough edges of the cut.

Smooth the gourd by twisting it back and forth on sandpaper until all the high and low places are evened out and the surface is completely plane.

Smooth the sharp outside edge of the cut, then apply glue to the cut edge and the sides of the gourd where the skin will touch it.

Position the skin on the gourd.

Put one staple into the skin and the gourd.

Stretch the skin taut to the opposite side.

Using your thumb, massage the skin until it is tight, pushing the skin outward. Then staple it to the gourd.

Set the staples with a hammer.

Tip: Be sure to stretch and pull the skin taut before each staple is applied. Pull tight, then staple. Go to the opposite side, pull tight, then staple.

Trim the skin.

Put glue on the edge band. *Artwork by Ginger Summit*

Gourd drum *Artwork by Mary McGregor*

for one hour or until pliable. Do not use hot water, as heat will render the natural hide glue, resulting in a sticky, limp material that will not tighten.

4. Ways to attach the drum head

a. *permanent*—Use glue and staples or upholstery tacks. As you secure the drum head to the body, massage it smooth around the edges. It is important to keep the tension even in all directions. As you work with the membrane, it will gradually stretch to conform to the shape of the gourd; while it is wet, it is quite flexible. Keep it taut and even as you massage and stretch it. When the membrane dries, it will shrink and become much tighter.

Resist the temptation to test the sound of the drum at this stage, since depressing the skin at all will create an uneven surface. Wait until the head is completely dry—at least 24 hours—before you begin to play it.

A drum head secured in this way on a gourd is permanent—that is, it can't be adjusted once it is fastened to the gourd. The tension will vary according to weather, humidity, and other environmental conditions such as temperature. If care has been taken in stretching the membrane, you will have a taut drum that will be very satisfactory.

b. *Tunable*

Materials

10-inch-diameter drum head preconstructed
    of plastic or rawhide, formed around a
    hoop

10-inch rings, the same diameter as the
    preconstructed drum head

4–6-inch ring for the base of the gourd,
    to secure the lashing

8–10-inch gourd—with a diameter that will
    fit the drum head

lacing, such as polyester cord or leather thong

Tools

saw

sandpaper

tapestry needle

A preconstructed drum head can be used on a gourd of the same diameter.

Fit a second ring on top of the preconstructed drum head to cinch it taut. In this case, an embroidery hoop was the right diameter.

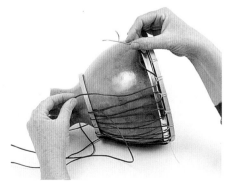

Temporary lacing between the embroidery hoop over the drum head and a smaller hoop at the base of the gourd will stabilize the top and bottom rings while they are being permanently laced.

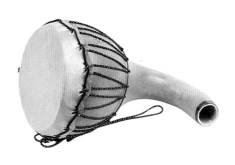

- holes in rawhide—Make holes around the circumference of the rawhide, and then while it is still damp, use a cord to lash it to a foundation at the base of the gourd. The foundation can be made of any material: a ring of metal or wood or a disk of leather that covers the base of the drum.
- lash hide to ring—Many adjustable tension drums have the head lashed to a hoop. This hoop can be a ring of metal, wrapped leather or cord, or even a wooden hoop. This holds the skin securely, distributes the tension evenly as the membrane is cinched tight, and gives the tension mechanism something firm to pull against. Many styles in many diameters are available ready-made at music stores.

c. *Double-headed drum*—By attaching more than one head to a single body, you can alter the resonance characteristics of the drum. The two heads will not sound much different, even though one head may be larger than the other, but the flexibility of the second head will affect the vibrations within the chamber. The heads can be attached separately using one of the methods already described; or they can be lashed together.

The heads can also be mounted on circular rings that are then lashed together. This technique is frequently used on both conical drum bodies and

The photos above and at the top of the page show four different drum-lacing patterns. *Artwork by Tim Delaney*

Lace two rings together.

After the lacing is as tight as possible, weave the end of the lacing thread horizontally through the variant threads by twisting the lacing before each intersection.

Laced drum *Artwork by Ginger Summit*

Right: Three drums, showing simple lacing directly through rawhide skin *Artwork by Jolee Schlea. Photo by Kirk Schlea*

Talking drum *Artwork by Ginger Summit*

Using turnbuckles instead of lacing *Artwork by Scott Johnson*

those with an hourglass shape. Double-headed, waisted drums are found throughout the world but are most familiar in West Africa and Japan. In Africa, one form of this drum is known as *kalunga* or "talking drum" because of the wide variety of sounds that can be coaxed from it by squeezing the lashing cords. The player holds the drum between his body and arm, squeezing the cords to increase the tension as he plays.

In Japan this style of drum is known as the *tsuzumi* and is commonly played in theater and dance performances that are accompanied by traditional musicians. Ornate colored satin cord secures the heads to the lacquered drum body.

While double-headed drums are usually made of carved wood cylinders or bowls, bottle gourds can be used very effectively. Either find a gourd that has two bulbs of similar size, or cut and join two bottle gourds at the neck to create an hourglass shape.

d. Drums may have an opening in the body, or can be left closed, depending on the preference of the musician. Frequently even drums that have two membranes also have an opening in the side to transmit sound.

Methods for Tuning a Drum

The drum head can be tuned either by modifying the mass or surface of the membrane itself or by adjusting the tension of the attachment. Some of the more common ways of adjusting the tension include:

- use of pegs or wedges under the lashing strings
- use of tuning beads, which can be slipped up the lashing, drawing them closer together

- use of separate lashing around the body of the drum, which cinches the lashing cords

In India, drums or *tabla* are an important part of musical ensembles, and it is critical that they are tuned precisely to complement the other instruments. In addition to adjusting the tension of the head, which is fitted on a ring and lashed to another ring lower on the body of the drum, a circle of black paste made of iron rust is frequently placed in the center of the drum head to increase the pitch. Water drums, which were common in many areas of North and Central America, rely on water inside the drum vessel to soak the membrane, keeping it soft and pliable during the performance.

In Africa, the sonority of the drum is enhanced by adding buzzers, made of metal disks or iron rings, to the outside of the drum, either attached to the membrane itself or to the lashing. These vibrate in sympathy and provide additional overtones, which are considered highly desirable.

Objects are frequently placed inside a drum as it is being constructed, for the same purpose: to add resonance. Many people in the northern part of Ghana put material inside a gourd for other reasons as well. A drum is thought to have a spirit, a soul, and a voice, just like other living things, including people. To ensure that the calabash drum has a proper "voice," the craftsman adds

- pebbles—from the yard of a talkative person in the village
- skin of a frog—so the membrane will remain supple
- bit of lion skin—so the drum will roar

In Africa, the pitch of each drum has significance beyond its acoustic properties. Drums are considered to have a power that extends well beyond their function as musical instruments. Frequently drums are thought to have gender: in a pair of drums, the male drum has a lower pitch and the female drum has a higher pitch. In a larger grouping, the mother and father drums or the elder drums have the lower pitches, and the son and daughter drums are smaller and respond in a higher-pitched chorus.

Making a Beater

An important element in creating the right sound with a drum is how the membrane is struck. The hand is the most flexible and versatile of beaters. The fingertips, the flat portion of the fingers, the side of the thumb, the palm, the heel, the side of the hand, even the elbow are used to create unparalleled variation on drums. A further advantage to using the hand is that the skin and flesh are not abrasive on the membrane. This not only affects the sound that is created, but the wear and tear on the membrane itself.

Even when a musician uses one hand to play the drum, he will often use another object to beat on the drum head as well. This most frequently is a

Wedges under lashing strip

Tuning beads, which slip up lashing to tighten skin

Separate cord around body of drum, cinching lashing cord

mallet/beater or a stick. Sticks generally are headless, whereas mallets and beaters have distinct heads, which may or may not be weighted. The materials used for the heads and the size can have a significant effect on the sound produced:

- Beaters that have a small striking surfaces will tend to emphasize higher frequencies. Larger striking surfaces will muffle the high frequencies and bring out the lower registers.
- Beaters with a hard surface will emphasize higher frequencies; softer surfaces will emphasize lower frequencies.

The weight of the mallet/beater and the material of the head should be matched to the head and body of the instrument for optimum resonance.

Beaters can be made of many different materials.

1. The beaters used in Africa are usually made from branches of trees or bushes. They often have an angle or arch and are held so the portion that strikes the membrane is directly perpendicular to the head and the movement of the tip of the beater is up and down. This is thought to be much easier on the membrane than a stroke from an oblique angle.

SOCIAL SIGNIFICANCE OF DRUMS

Drums and the sounds they produce have come to assume significance that varies with nearly every culture in which they are played. In some cultures drums and the musicians who play them are simply a part of the noisy cacophony of daily life. In other cultures, drums are considered so sacred that they have special buildings where they reside and are cared for, and only specially designated musicians are allowed to play them. Within these two extremes are many fascinating customs and beliefs, each reflecting the diverse societies that still color our world.

In India, drums can be played by either men or women, although they are usually played by men. In ancient times musicians usually came from the lower classes or castes, and drummers were no exception. Today musicians who specialize in the drum or *tabla,* which may be played solo or in accompaniment for the sitar or other instrument ensembles, are highly respected members of society.

Historically, the European and Western musical tradition placed a much greater emphasis on melody and virtuosity on instruments that play melodic lines. Drums and other percussion instruments traditionally received no special recognition or attention. This attitude is changing today, as drummers in popular musical groups are not only respected but highly revered!

In stark contrast, African music places a heavy emphasis on rhythmic elements of music and a wide variety of percussion sounds. The instruments and the musicians who play them are held in great esteem, and in some societies the instruments themselves are regarded as sacred.

Drums have also played a very important role in the music of Native American cultures. Often the drum and rattle are the only instruments used to accompany ceremonies and dance.

Some examples of drum beaters *Artwork by Ginger Summit*

2. Make a beater from a piece of hardwood dowel. The diameter of the dowel should be matched to the drum—the smaller the drum, the lighter the dowel. Sand completely, so it is completely smooth in your hands, and cover the tip with any of the following. Each cover will produce a different sound, so experiment with several.

- a wad of rubber bands
- sa tight wrap of yarn
- foam rubber
- cloth or felt strips wound around the dowel
- a woolly ball made of fleece
- a champagne cork
- a wooden ball or a bead, or a drawer pull
- a brush
- a Super-Ball
- a circle of rubber tire

The first five materials can each be wrapped tightly around the end of the drumstick and fastened in place with glue or electrical tape, or securely tied with dental floss or string. A woolly ball of fleece can be wrapped with a circle of cloth and then tied securely to the drumstick.

A Super-Ball makes a wonderfully resilient mallet that has minimal negative impact on the drum membrane. It can be purchased in many sizes. Take care when drilling the hole that will be used to fasten it to the dowel. Begin with a very small diameter hole, gradually increasing the size of the drill bit until the hole is slightly smaller than the end of the stick. Taper the stick end slightly, and gently twist it inside the ball. Before it is completely in place, put some glue on the join to keep the ball in place.

Clapper Drum Rattles: *Matracas*

Matracas, or clapper drums, are a type of small drum held in one hand and shaken or twisted much like a rattle. Membranes usually cover both sides of the frame, which is attached to a handle. Small beads are strung to the frame loosely and strike the membrane when the instrument is spun about. The hollow frames

Materials

short-handled dipper gourd

rawhide skin

cord to lace drum heads, secure beads

beads

decorative braid

Tools

saw

tapestry needle

sandpaper

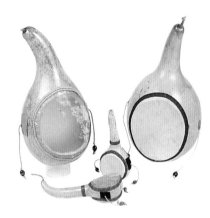

Matracas Artwork by Sue Westhues

for these little noisemakers can easily be made from a small dipper or bottle gourd.

1. Slice two sides off the bulb and cut two membranes slightly bigger than the openings in the gourd. Soak the membranes.
2. Punch holes in the membranes, making sure that they have the same number of holes.
3. Before you attach the membranes, make small holes in the center of both sides of the gourd frame and string a length (approximately eight inches) of waxed linen from each opening.
4. Attach the membranes to the gourd by stitching them together around the gourd frame.
5. After the membranes are dry, attach beads to the strings that were inserted into the sides of the gourd frame long enough to slap the membrane as the instrument is shaken or twisted.

The instrument is played by rolling the handle between the palms of the hands.

Friction Drum

A completely different type of instrument that is included in the classification of membranophone is the friction drum. Different forms are found in many parts of the world—Asia, Europe, Brazil, Central America, and throughout sub-Saharan Africa.

This instrument originated in Gabon, West Africa, and the Congo region, where it is still played. The body is basically a drum made of a gourd with a membrane covering one end. A stick is fastened in the center of the membrane so that it hangs down through the body of the gourd. To play, one hand is coated with resin to rub the stick, and the other hand dampens the membrane head to modify the sound. In many tribes, including the Zulu in South Africa, this

Right: Top of a Brazilian *cuica* drum.

Far right: Inside a Brazilian *cuica* drum, with a wood dowel attached to the skin instead of cordage

instrument is used as part of rituals, such as initiation and mourning.

In the Ivory Coast, the instrument is used to imitate the panther. It is played during ceremonies in which certain spirits, represented by the panther, are called to the village.

The friction drum is also found in South and Central America, where it is known as a *cuica*. It is probably most familiar to musicians and dancers as an important instrument in samba and bossa nova groups. In one particular mountainous area of Mexico, the sound created by rubbing the leather thong in the *cuica* was used to imitate the jaguar.

In Europe an adaptation of this instrument became known as a *rommelpot* and was a common part of the Twelfth Night festivities. The body was constructed of wood, the membrane made of pig bladder, and the stick cut from elder wood. Traveling musicians would play this instrument as they wandered through the towns, singing for money and food.

Two kazoos, showing membrane

Noneke / Kazoo

Many of us are familiar with the kazoo, which distorts the singing voice by vibrating a piece of paper held between the lips or a short distance away. Children often create impromptu instruments by placing waxed paper over a comb and then humming or singing to cause the paper to vibrate.

Many instruments, particularly in Africa, use this same principle to create a buzzing noise in addition to the instrument sound. This has already been described in the construction of the *mbira* and the xylophone, where spider-egg casing or a thin gut membrane is stretched over an opening in the gourd resonator. Such a device is called a *miriliton*.

A simple kazoo using a gourd and a vibrating membrane is called a *noneke* in Africa.

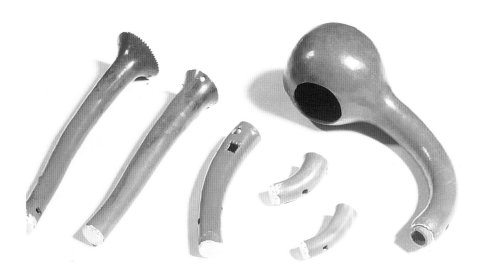

Left: Malipenga gourd kazoos, from the Cewa people of Malawi. These kazoos are used to accompany the *Malipenga* dance with drums, which parodies a military drill. The dancer sings into the hole nearest the membrane. The length of the longest straight one is 13.5 inches. *Photo by fine arts students, Rhodes University From the collection of the International Library of African Music, Rhodes University, Grahamstown, South Africa*

Kazoo

Materials	Tools
narrow gourd or neck of gourd	saw
	sandpaper
waxed paper	glue
decorative braid	awl

Clean out the inside of a gourd neck.

Cut the gourd.

Cut a piece of waxed paper larger than the opening in the gourd.

Spread glue on the cut edge of the gourd.

Using finger pressure, tighten the wax paper membrane to glue it to the gourd.

Apply glue to the edge of the membrane.

Press two parts of the kazoo together with the membrane inside.

Use masking tape to hold the two glued halves together.

File a small hole in the mouthpiece side of the membrane ⅜ inch before the membrane.

Hum, with mouth open, into the end of the gourd. *Artwork by Ginger Summit Project inspired by Sue Westhues*

A very thin skin is loosely stretched over the end of a conical-shaped gourd tube and secured. In Africa this membrane was frequently spider-egg casing or stomach lining of sheep or cows, but waxed paper makes an easy substitute.

An unusual instrument that functions much like a kazoo but does not use a vibrating membrane is a *mataphono,* found in Uruguay and Paraguay. It is made of a small canteen gourd. The gourd is cut in half, a hole is made on one side, and a leather washer is glued to hold both halves together. By humming or singing into the hole, the musician makes the two halves of the gourd vibrate together, amplifying and distorting the sound.

Mataphono. A half-inch hole is made on one side with a leather hinge glued to hold both halves together, and a tiny hole, ¹⁄₁₆ inch, is made on the opposite side.

Part 3

Chordophones

Chordophones are instruments for which the sound source is a vibrating string. To produce a vibration, a string must be held taut, so two important elements of the instruments in this category are the string or strings, and a rigid frame. Most chordophones also have a sound-board with a surface to which the vibrations of the string are transferred, thereby increasing the effective vibration, and a resonating box that amplifies the volume of the sound produced. These components have been combined throughout history in many ways, which can be broken down into five basic subcategories:

- The musical bow has one or more strings attached to a curved stick. In its most simple form a portion of the bow is held or braced against a resonator temporarily while it is being played to increase the volume of sound produced. Sometimes this resonator is as simple as the mouth or chest cavity. Other times it is a container, usually a gourd. In several instances one or more resonating chambers are attached permanently to the bow.
- Harps are instruments in which a set of strings rise in a plane perpendicular to the sound box. Usually the strings pass through holes or an open space in the upper surface of the sound box and attach to the bowed or arched neck above.
- The lyre has two arms that extend from the sound box parallel to its surface, with a crossbar holding the arms apart at the upper end. The strings extend across the surface of the sound box to the crossbar at the outer ends of the arms.
- The lute family has a single neck that extends on the same plane as the upper surface of the sound box. The strings stretch across from the one edge

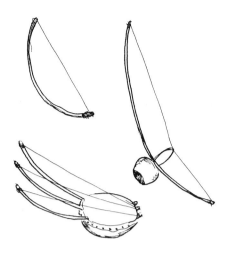

Left to right: Simple bow *berimbau,* simple bow with gourd resonator, pluriarc (three bows on one gourd resonator)

of the sound box, over a bridge, and along the length to the farthest end of the neck.

- Zithers are similar to the lute, except that the sound box itself is elongated with the strings stretched along the entire length of the instrument body. The strings are raised from the surface by one or more bridges.

Adjusting the tension

The first consideration is the means for holding the string under tension. It must be held taut, but also must be allowed to vibrate freely through all or part of its length. Strings can be attached to the instrument body in various ways. The simplest solution is simply to tie or fasten the cord to the frame. This is fine for instruments with a flexible frame, such as a *gopiyantra* or musical bow. But such a permanent attachment cannot be tuned or adjusted easily, so many techniques have evolved to tighten or loosen the tension on the string.

A simple and very traditional technique is to wrap a strip of leather or other fabric tightly around a part of the framework, to which one end of the string is attached. By turning, twisting, or moving this ring on the framework, the tension on the string and therefore the pitch is controlled. This mechanism, while not precise, requires frequent adjustment as it tends to slip during a performance, but it has been used for centuries in the construction of many instruments.

Another solution commonly found on stringed instruments today is a tuning peg, or pin.

A screw eye, which is screwed directly into the neck or frame of the instrument, is the very simplest kind of tuning pin. For a beginning project, this may be a very satisfactory technique to use. By tying the string to a screw eye at one or both ends of the instrument, the tension can be increased by a simple turn of the screw.

A wide variety of tuning pegs are available at music stores that carry stringed instruments. Or you can make your own: Start with dowels ¼–⅜ inch in diameter. File and sand one end of the dowel to a slight taper. Drill a hole in the neck of the instrument slightly smaller than the dowel. Shape the hole with a rat-tail file that has a slight taper. This will allow for a precise fit of the peg. A wood or ceramic bead glued to the end of the dowel will provide a grip when turning or adjusting it.

Much more complex tuning mechanisms are made for guitars, banjos, and zithers. They come in a variety of styles, sizes, and prices. Look at the options available in a complete music supply store, and purchase the tuning mechanism before you start to make your instrument. Some mechanisms are mounted on the side of the neck, while others are mounted from the rear. Dimensions of these tuning devices vary considerably, and you want to know these before you begin constructing your instrument.

Controlling the length of string vibration

Since length of string directly affects the pitch, some stringed instruments have many strings of different lengths, each of which is designed to play a single note. Examples of this are harps, zithers, and pianos. But in other instruments, the length of the string is adjusted continuously as it is being played, so a single string can effectively be used to sound many notes. Some examples of this are guitars, violins, and mountain dulcimers.

The string vibrates between two points of contact, where it is free. In some instruments, this is actually the entire length of the string, from the place it is attached to the instrument body on one end to the tuning peg or place of attachment on the other. But length can be effectively shortened by inserting a surface over which the string must cross. This surface has two different names, depending on which end of the string it is located near. The surface nearest the tuning peg is called the "nut." This is usually permanently mounted on the neck or body of the instrument, so that the string must pass over this before being turned on the tuning peg. The raised surface at the other end of the string is called a "bridge." This provides the direct contact between the string and the resonator or soundboard. The bridge has two functions: the first is to hold the string above the sound box and transfer the vibrations directly to it; the second is to define one (or more) of the parameters of the length of the string. Often in chordophones, the bridge is fixed (as in most lutes, lyres, and some harps), but in many zithers the bridges can be adjusted for accurate tuning of individual notes. In some zithers, such as the *koto* (Japan), each individual string has a moveable bridge that is adjusted before playing.

A string can also be temporarily stopped or shortened by pressing or pinching it with a finger (as in spiked or pierced fiddles), or by pressing the string against the neck, as in a violin or cello, or a fret, such as in the guitar and banjo.

Mass, or thickness, of the string

The strings themselves can be made of many types of material. Historically, they have been made of materials that are most readily available, such as plant fibers, silk, and gut. Today, these are all gradually being replaced because of inherent weaknesses: plant fibers tend to wear quickly under constant abrasion, and both silk and gut are stretchy and "give" in moist conditions. Nylon and various metals, including brass and steel, are the most popular types of string used today. The material of the string, how it is constructed, and its thickness all influence the way it will vibrate—affecting not only the pitch but also the overtones. Strings of nylon, steel, and gut are available in many different diameters and lengths in most musical instrument stores. Some are single strands, while others are compound, woven, or wrapped. For instruments that have more than one string, it is important that tension be uniform, or nearly so, across all the strings. Therefore, try to match strings with each other, their intended pitch range, and the dimensions of the instrument. As you create your own instrument, experiment not only with commercial products but also with materials you find around your home, such as wire, rubber, cotton, or even plant materials, to see the sounds they produce.

HOW A STRING VIBRATES

The distinguishing characteristic of chordophones is the sound produced by one or more vibrating strings. Before considering other factors, such as body shape and details of construction, it is important to be aware of some simple acoustic principles of a vibrating string.

An activated string vibrates not only as a whole, but also in sections. The longest vibration is the primary vibration, which determines the pitch, or the fundamental. The shorter or partial vibrations create the overtones, or the harmonics.

The pitch, or fundamental vibration, can be affected in several ways:

- The tension or tightness of the string—increased tension raises the pitch.

- The length of the string—the shorter the string, the higher the pitch (and conversely, the longer the string, the lower the pitch).

- Thickness of the string—the greater the mass of the string, the lower the pitch. When using more than one string on an instrument, it is important to keep the tension approximately equal between them. Therefore, strings of different thicknesses or composition frequently will be used on a single instrument to create a wider range of tones while keeping the tension equal.

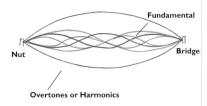

1. The fundamental is determined by the length of the string.
2. Selective harmonies amplified by the resonator add tone "color."

There are many different ways the string can be sounded, or made to vibrate. The most common ways are plucking, either with the fingers or a plectrum (or pick), or bowing. The string will vibrate at the same pitch whether bowed or plucked, but the bow allows for continuous tone. Occasionally the strings are hammered, as in many zithers and the piano, for example, or tapped with a stick, as with musical bows. A variety of materials have been used to make a plectrum, including a flat stone, coin, shell, plastic, and wire. Each will have a slightly different effect on the tone produced, so experiment to find a material that creates a sound that is pleasing to you.

Purpose and Function of the Resonator or Sound Box

Because the string itself has such a small surface area, the vibrations it causes in the surrounding air are frequently inaudible. By making contact with a resonator or sound box, the vibrations are amplified dramatically. In most chordophones, the framework that holds the strings under tension can be thought of as separate from the resonating chamber. Although they are attached and frequently integrated with each other, they perform two different functions, and the individual elements of each function should be considered separately when constructing your own instrument.

(Some instruments in the zither category are different: that is, the structure that holds the strings taut, such as the dulcimer or zither, is often hollow and functions as a resonator as well.)

In the chordophones where the strings cross the surface of the resonator (i.e., lute, lyre, and zither families), the string must be slightly raised from the surface of the sound box while still maintaining a direct contact so that the vibration of the string will be transferred to the resonator. Various styles of bridges have been designed for this purpose, which either lift strings individually or all the strings together. Bridges have been made of almost any material that is solid and will transfer vibrations without excessively damping or distorting them. The height of the bridge varies from the very tall bridge in the harp-zither (e.g., the *kora,* or hunter's harp), to a simple wire or stick used in some lutes. A bridge can be permanently attached to the soundboard, or it can simply be held in place by pressure or the tension of the strings.

The size, shape, and material of the resonator, as well as how it is attached to the framework supporting the strings, all affect the relative prominence of the overtones and harmonics of the fundamental pitch, but not the pitch itself (which is established by the vibrating string). A smaller sound box will resonate the higher frequencies more, while the larger box will emphasize the lower vibrations. The shape also affects how the sounds are transmitted to the surrounding air and thus to the listener. The naturally round shape of the gourd is particularly suited to reflect frequencies evenly, but the inner surface should be treated with polyurethane or other sealer to reduce the damping effects of the soft and porous inner shell. In some chordophones, the resonator is an open vessel such as the musical bow, where the inverted gourd is left open. In others, the resonator body is enclosed with a membrane or a solid surface, such as a thin piece of wood. When a membrane is used, it is usually rawhide of some small animal.

There is usually a hole or series of holes in the body of the resonator to allow the vibrations to escape. While this is particularly important if the sound surface is rigid, such as a thin piece of wood, resonators that are covered with a membrane can also have holes. These can be either in the top surface or anywhere in the body of the sound box.

Musical Bow

The musical bow is most likely the ancestor of stringed instruments. It is but a small step from the zing of the bow in a hunt, to the strum of the string back in the camp, recounting the thrill of the adventure.

Simple, Detached Resonator

The simplest form of musical bow is played by holding it against the mouth to resonate the sound created as the string is strummed. These were popular throughout Africa, northern Mexico, and later the southeastern United States, where the mouth bow is still a part of Appalachian music traditions.

Often the bow is placed on a resonator such as a gourd as it is being played. This type of musical bow is found in many forms throughout Africa. One example is the *kichikalangal,* played by the Woloff tribe in West Africa.

Attached Resonator

The next level of musical bow has an attached resonator, as in the Congo region and along the west coast of Africa, where a gourd is attached to the bow by means of a loop of sinew, string, or wire. This form of the instrument was transported to Brazil and Central America by slaves in the 16th century. It is now called the *berimbau.* It is still an important instrument in Brazil as the accompaniment to *capoeira,* a form of skilled fighting somewhat related to karate or judo. It began as a form of physical training within the slave quarters in Brazil. With the addition of music and song, plantation owners were unaware of their slaves' planning rebellion while seemingly innocently dancing. *Capoeira* is still a very important activity in Brazil, and has rapidly gained popularity in the United States. The physical movements and music have been standardized by several prominent leaders, who have founded schools with studios in most large cities. The music and movement are closely interrelated, the music acting as an energizing power that maintains the pace and momentum of the dancer/fighter. Both the *berimbau* and the *caxixi* rattle, which is played with it, are becoming familiar instruments worldwide.

The instrument is usually held in one hand parallel to the body with the

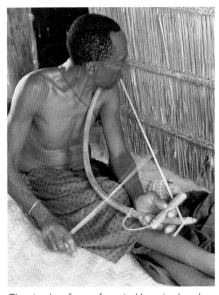

The simplest form of musical bow is played by being held against the mouth, which resonates the sound created as the string is struck. From The Gambia. *Photo by David Gamble*

The bow is placed on a resonator such as a gourd as it is being played. From The Gambia. *Photo by David Gamble*

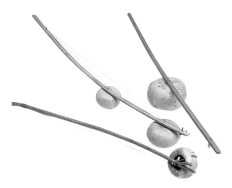

Artwork from left to right: *Berimbau,* double-strung bow, mouth bow. The double-strung bow can achieve three tones from the single string. The gourd resonator in the center of the bow slides along the bow, varying the vibrating lengths of one string. The bow can be plucked or struck, played as a two-string mouth bow or a two-string *berimbau,* using either mouth or gourd as primary resonator. The traditional mouth-resonated bow with a removable gourd demonstrates the effect of an additional resonator on the volume of the instrument. *Artwork by Tony Pizzo Photo by Fletcher Manley*

This eight-foot-long musical bow is actually two sticks (double otate) wired together and attached to a gourd resonator. The Tepehuanes, Coras, and Huichols play this instrument. The resonator rests on a platform on the ground and the rawhide strings are beaten with sticks on either side of the resonator to create at least two pitches. *Artwork by Xavier Quijas Yxayotl*

Chimvokomvoko bowed bow or fiddle played by Shona/Karanga children, Zimbabwe *Photo by fine arts students, Rhodes University From the collection of the International Library of African Music, Rhodes University, Grahamstown, South Africa*

string outside and the gourd next to the chest. As the string is tapped with a stick, the resonator is pulsed against the chest in a rhythm that accompanies the songs or dancing. The pitch is further modified by the use of a stone or coin held in the fingers of the hand that holds the bow. The coin is pressed against the string at various positions along its length, thereby effectively shortening the vibration.

A related bow from Africa has notches carved in the bow itself. Rubbing another stick across the notches causes the string to vibrate, which is then amplified by the attached gourd. (See photograph below left.)

The *celebau,* played in a sitting position with the gourd between the feet, is a louder instrument because the string is in direct contact with the gourd. The string is passed under the wooden dowel that runs through the top of the gourd. *Artwork by Salih Qawi*

Two-string mouth bow with additional gourd resonator. Used by Indians in Sonora, Mexico. *Artwork by Leigh Adams*

Chizambi friction mouth bow and rattle stick of the Shona/Karanga people of Zimbabwe. With the palm leaf string held in front of your open mouth, rub the rattle stick along the serrations on the bow to make the string vibrate. The vibrations are then amplified by the attached gourd. Length: 19 inches. *Photo by fine arts students, Rhodes University From the collection of the International Library of African Music, Rhodes University, Grahamstown, South Africa*

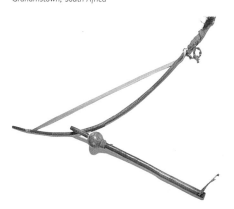

Above: Tools and materials: gourd riffler rasps, straight rasp stick (*beriba* wood), piano wire, leather scraps, 1.25-inch nails, hammer, saw, old tire (an optional source of wire)

Right: Test *beriba* wood and find the flexibility to see if it will hold the pitch. If it's too weak, it won't hold the pitch and will continue to bend. If it's too strong, it can't be bent.

Berimbau

Materials	Tools
stick—6 feet long (*beriba* wood or ash preferable)	saw
	hammer
piano wire—7 feet	files
nails	sandpaper
small leather pieces	scissors
gourd—6-inch diameter	
palm oil or leather dye	
cotton string	

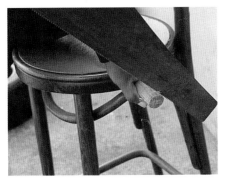

Make the initial cut for the foot (*pe*) of the *berimbau* and mark the notched end with a saw cut.

Use a rasp to cut and shape the foot. Make a distinct wall for it.

Smooth the edges of the head of the *berimbau* so it's rounded and protects the sides from splintering. Scrape away the hairy bark fibers that would otherwise clog the sandpaper. Use a rasp to shave down any knots and finish removing bark.

Sand the wood with coarse sandpaper (80-grit), followed by 120-grit. Do a final sanding with 220-grit (extra-fine) sandpaper.

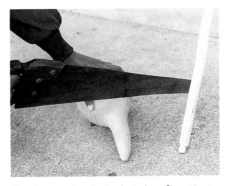

Cut the gourd to fit the *berimbau*. Sometimes the top of the gourd can be used for a smaller *berimbau* of higher pitch (viola).

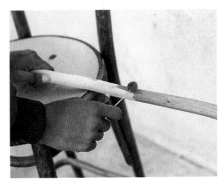

Stain the wood.

Use a file to smooth the edges of the gourd

A leather circle is used to protect the wood from the wire string cutting into it. (Also, without the leather the instrument will have a more metallic sound.) Glue the leather to the wood. Nail two 1.5-inch brads through the leather into the wood to keep the leather from spinning.

The traditional Brazilian way of obtaining wire for a *berimbau*, using a sharp hunting knife to remove several rounds of wire from an old tire, a very difficult and dangerous process. Hours of scraping rubber off the wire will still be necessary even after the wire is freed.

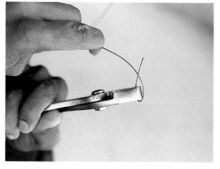

Bend a loop in one end of the piano wire just large enough to go over the tenon of the foot of the *berimbau*. Twist the end of the wire around the base of the loop to hold it in place.

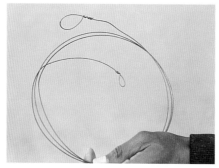

Make a smaller loop at the other end of the wire.

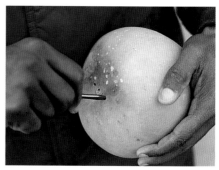

Place the stick on the bottom of the gourd and make two holes in the gourd on either side of the stick. Sand slightly to flatten the stick about six inches where the gourd will be attached, so as much surface area as possible of the stick is touching the gourd.

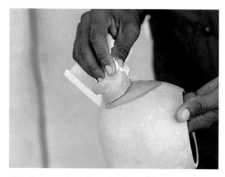

Oil the gourd with red palm oil (*ten ten tai*) or decorate it.

Pass the string through two holes in a piece of leather on the inside of the gourd. The leather protects the gourd from splitting from the pressure of the string.

Pass the string through the two holes in the gourd and make a loop on the back of the gourd that will allow just three fingers to pass through. The loop should be big enough for the gourd to fit over the stick, and there should be a little space so you can manipulate the stone against the wire. Tie the ends of the string with a square knot.

Attach a 24-inch length of string to the small loop in the wire. To attach the wire to the stick, slip the leather washer over the tenon to protect the wood, then the large wire loop over the tenon on the foot.

Bring the wire over the leather nailed to the head of the *berimbau* and down the back of the *berimbau*. Use your thigh to help bend the wood. Don't overbend or you'll break the stick.

Another way to bring the wire over the leather and down the back of the *berimbau*. Use your foot to get the stick to bend sufficiently. Be careful not to overbend and break your stick.

Bring the wire down and wrap it around the stick and then continue to wrap the string around the stick with a half hitch to set the wire in place. To secure it, continue to wrap the string around the stick and then finish it off with another half hitch.

About one hand length from the end is the preferred position for the gourd in *Capoeira*. In West Africa the gourd might be found at the middle of the bow. Some performers like to put the gourd in such a position on the wire that the tone of the string is an even octave above the tone on the other side of the gourd.

Slip the string loop at the bottom of the gourd around the foot of the *berimbau*. Squeeze the wire and *berimbau* together so you can slide the gourd on. Always squeeze the wire to adjust the position of the gourd for the pitch.

Tip: When you first make the *berimbau*, don't bend the wood too much, or the tone will be in the lower register. Leave the *berimbau* strung at this tension for a week. Afterward, loosen the string and restring it a little more tightly. In this way your wood will adjust gradually to the tension and not crack as a result of being overbent initiallly.

This photo shows the location of the holes in the gourd in relation to the wood. Notice that the distance between the holes is exactly the same as the diameter of the wood. This provides the tightest fit of the gourd on the stick.

Playing the *berimbau*. A coin or stone is touching the string, thereby changing the pitch while the right hand holds the beating stick and the *caxixi* rattle. The gourd itself is held against the body for a muffled sound.

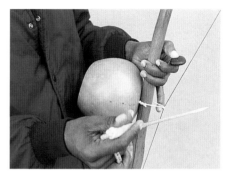

The left hand is holding the coin (stone) away from the string and the gourd is away from the body, creating a louder sound. If the gourd is pulled away from the body just after the string is hit, a "wow-wow" sound is produced. *Artwork by Salih Qawi*

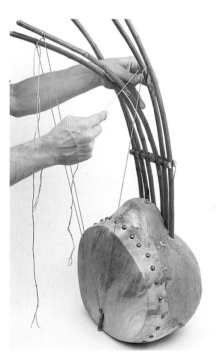

Tie each individual string to the tailpiece (bridge) and then tie the other end to the midsection of a bow arm. Do this for each of the six strings. The three bass strings will be in the middle. The lighter strings will be toward the outside. *Artwork by Geof Morgan*

Multiple Bows (Pluriarc)

Another variation of musical bow combines several separate bows attached to a single resonator, which is often a large gourd. (This form is known as a pluriarc.) The appearance is similar to fingers extending from a palm, each finger controlling the tension and the length of an individual string.

This is related to a harp, except that each string is held in tension by its own bow, each bow producing a different pitch. This type of instrument is found primarily in the Congo region of Central Africa, where it is known as a *lukombe* (Central Africa) or *nsambi* (Gabon/Angola).

Lyres

A group of instruments that was popular in many forms during Greek and Roman times is the lyre. Today it is rarely seen, except in Africa among the tribes that were heavily influenced by the Muslims, in the north and down the eastern portion of the continent.

The main components of a lyre are a sound box, which supports a framework of two arms that extend upward, parallel to the surface of the resonator. The strings extend from the base of the sound box over a bridge to a crossbar, which separates the two arms.

Some crossbars are equipped with tuning pegs, or rings, although in most examples of old or popular instruments gut strings are simply wound around the bar. In Europe the strings of some lyres were bowed, but in most other cultures and in Africa today the strings are plucked either with the fingers or with a plectrum.

Most lyres have seven strings, although they may have as few as three or as many as 20.

Many materials have been used for the sound box: wood, gourd, turtle shell, even a human skull. Those constructed with wooden sound boxes tend to be

Historical photo of a man playing the lyre in the Belgian Congo *Photo by Herbert Lang. Photo courtesy of the Department of Library Services, American Museum of Natural History, July 1911*

associated with religious festivals or use by nobility. The popular instruments are used for entertainment at festivals and are usually made with gourds.

The body of the instruments can be decorated with shells and beads that jingle, creating a buzzing noise as the instrument is played.

While most of the popular lyres are relatively small and can be played braced on the lap or against the chest, the *obukano* lyre of Ethiopia is quite large. It has eight to 12 strings, and may have an overall length up to 3½ feet, with a resonator over 18 inches in diameter. It has been described as the "double bass" of East Africa.

Lyres are frequently used to accompany singing in religious festivals or ceremonies associated with healing.

Traditional Kenyan lyre *From the collection of Gerry Flewharty*

Lyre

Materials

gourd—10–12-inch diameter

rawhide skin

tacks, decorative

2 arms, approximately ¾-inch diameter, each approximately 18 inches long

crossbar—approximately ¾-inch diameter and approximately 12 inches long

glue

heavy waxed linen

strings—nylon, gut, or waxed linen

Tools

saw

sandpaper

scraper

leather awl

hammer

knife

Scrape the inside of the gourd resonator.

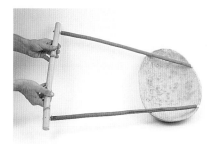

Check the accuracy of the frame's angle and size in relation to the gourd.

Notched vertical supports fit the hole in the horizontal bar.

Make holes for tacks all around the skin prior to fastening. Holes should be about one and a half to two inches apart.

Apply glue to the edge of the skin that will be in contact with the gourd resonator and the lip of the gourd.

Push the tack through the hole in the skin and into the gourd.

After the first tack is pushed into the gourd, go to the opposite side, pull the skin very taut, and push the tack in through the hole previously made in the skin.

The skin is now attached at opposite ends midway between the tacks. Now pull the skin and push the tack as before. Continue all around the gourd until there are tacks approximately every two inches.

Smooth the skin against the gourd. Add more glue if necessary or wet a portion of the skin again to make it more flexible if it is drying too quickly. This step will take time.

Indicate where to make the entry cuts and mark.

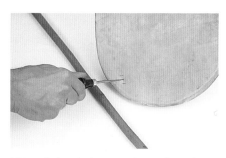

Make a hole right between the marks with an awl.

Enlarge the hole to accommodate the end of the arm.

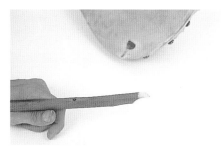

Note the profile of the end of the arm. It has been cut with a lip that will fit on the edge of the gourd shell under the skin.

Insert the arms into the hole in the skin with a twisting motion. Push both arms all the way until the flat part of the cut rests on top of the edge of the gourd under the skin.

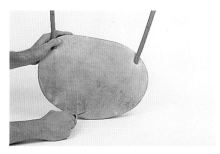

With an awl, punch a hole in the skin equidistant from the arms and very close to the bottom edge of the gourd but about three quarters of an inch away.

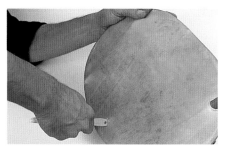

Enlarge the hole in the skin. The handle of an inexpensive flat paintbrush works very well.

Put the awl through the hole at an angle and make a hole in the front face of the gourd.

Enlarge the hole in the gourd with a knife blade.

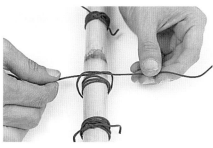

Using a heavy waxed linen twine, tie a clove hitch onto the horizontal bar that connects the arms. Then tie the ends together in a series of square knots until the ends are used up.

Attach the strings to the rings, one string per ring.

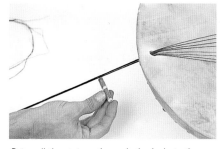

Bring all the strings through the hole in the skin and then through the matching hole in the gourd.

Notch a small piece of wood that will be the tailpiece and carefully tie all the strings around the tailpiece using one square knot.

Pull up the slack in the strings by turning the rings on the horizontal bar. By turning the rings you will tighten any slack in the string.

When playing the lyre, one hand is in front and one hand is behind the strings. You may carve a bridge to lift the strings away from the skin just above their exit from the skin. *Artwork by Geof Morgan*

Harps

The classification of chordophones identified as "harp" includes instruments in which the strings are held upright from the resonating chamber in a plane perpendicular to the soundboard or membrane.

Most of us are familiar with the European style of harp, where the sound box is integral with the rigid framework supporting the strings, and frequently is carved or made of wood. Variations of this style are found in many cultures around the world (notably Europe and South America), and tend to be used in more formal musical presentations. Many other instruments considered to be harps are found primarily in Africa. They can be subclassified as "arched," "angular," or "forked."

Arched

The arched type is generally felt to be a direct evolution of the musical bow, and one form is sometimes called the bow harp. These harps have a long, curved neck, with one end anchored in the sound box. The box is usually a container, such as a gourd, which has been covered with a membrane.

The strings are made from hide, tendon, vine, raffia, or fishing line, or occasionally spun from tail hairs of animals such as giraffe. The number of strings may range from one to 10.

The strings are attached to the base of the bow inside the resonator. They pass through holes in the membrane and connect to the upper end of the arched bow at intervals, so that the strings have different vibrating lengths and give different pitches. Frequently, tuning pegs are set into the bow to allow strings to be tuned individually. However, the tension on each string will affect the other strings since they are all anchored on a flexible bow, so the tuning is not precise. When played, the harp is usually held with the strings facing either upright or downward to the ground, but it can also be held on its side so that the strings are parallel to the ground, depending on the tradition of the culture.

African harp

Harp *Artwork by Liz Was*

Forked/Frame Harp

Another shape is the forked or frame harp in which a triangular frame is made with wood pieces such as a forked branch. One of the corners, such as the main branch, extends into the resonating box. Because it is familiar throughout the west coast of Africa, there are many names, such as *kanin, gambareh,* and *loma* harp.

Harps frequently serve as percussion as well as stringed instruments. Buzzers are attached to many different parts of the harp to create a distinctive sound. Rings or metal can be attached to the framework where the strings are attached, spider-egg cases are stretched across openings in the resonator, and pellets are even placed within the sound box. On some occasions, second musicians actually tap on the base of the harp either to keep pace with the beat or to create a counter-rhythm.

Harp *Artwork and photo by Alberto Magnin*

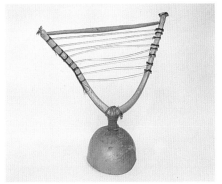

Liberian forked harp *Photo by Ginger Summit. From the Treganza Anthropology Museum, San Francisco State University*

Contemporary musicians have made harps in many different configurations, frequently using gourds as the resonator.

Harp-zither (*Mvet*)

Two other important instruments can be classified as harp, but share characteristics of other categories as well. One is the *mvet* (or *muet*), which is sometimes called a harp-zither. It consists of a length of bamboo stalk to which a continuous string has been strung back and forth several times along its length. It is passed through notches on a tall bridge that is situated at the midpoint of the stalk, holding the strings upright and parallel to the stalk. On the opposite side of the stalk one to three gourds are attached to amplify the sounds. As the musician sings and plucks the strings, he pulses one of the calabash against his chest. This is an important instrument for the pygmies in the Congo region as well as

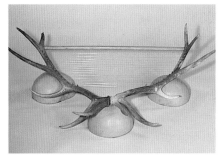

Top: Tenor elk harp *Artwork by Bill and Mary Buchen Photo by Robert Nash*

Bottom: Harp *Artwork by Bill and Mary Buchen Photo by Robert Nash*

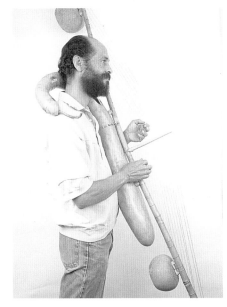

Above: *Mvet Artwork and photo by Arthur Stephens*

Right: *Mvet Artwork by Robert Hilton*

Top: African hunter's harp

Bottom: *Cora* from the Malenke tribe, Mali
From the collection of Ginger Summit

Top right: *Cora* player in Mali *Photo by Beany Wezelman*

southern Cameroon, northern Gabon, and Central African Republic. The player of this instrument is similar to the *griot* in other communities. He combines the function of musician, dancer, and storyteller, keeping the cultural history alive through his performances.

Kora

The *kora*, considered by many to be one of the most beautiful-sounding instruments in Africa, can be classified either as a harp or as a lute (and occasionally called a harp-lute). It consists of a sound box, which is a very large calabash, through which is fastened a long, cylindrical wood neck. The calabash is covered with a skin stretched over the top and extending down the outer walls of the gourd. The membrane is traditionally held securely in place by decorative nails in fancy patterns. One or more holes are cut in the side of the calabash to allow the sounds to escape. These holes are also used to receive "gifts" of money from an appreciative audience. Two handles of wood sticks shorter than the neck are mounted through the top membrane and braced securely against the lower surface of the gourd. A mounting piece is secured to the bottom end of the neck, to which 21 strings are tied. These are then stretched over a tall bridge and secured to tuning rings that are evenly spaced along the length of the neck. The bridge is approximately eight inches in height and at least two inches wide, with notches on either side. This bridge holds the strings perpendicular to the surface of the resonator in two rows of 10 and 11 cords.

The *kora* can also have metal disks attached to the top of the bridge and occasionally along the periphery of the membrane to create a distinctive buzz.

The player holds the instrument by the handles braced against his abdomen or upright on the ground in front of him, with his middle and little fingers (third, fourth, and fifth fingers) wrapped securely around the handles. This leaves the thumb and index fingers free to pluck the strings. Although the shape of the instrument is that of a lute, the arrangement of the strings on the bridge and the manner in which it is played by plucking cause it to be classified as a harp.

The *kora* is an exceptionally beautiful instrument, not only to see but also to hear. It is played as a solo instrument, as an accompaniment for a singer, or as part of an ensemble combined with one or more instruments.

The *kora* is very popular throughout an area that includes Guinea, Gambia, Senegal, Mali, Burkina Faso, Ivory Coast, and Nigeria, where it is also known as a *cora, corah, kooraa, soron,* and *bolon.* In Guinea there is a 19-string *kora* that is called a *seron.* Several other related instruments exist in West Africa with fewer strings, ranging from 10 to 19. The *bolongbato* was an early form of the instrument with only four strings, played before battle to encourage the warriors.

As with many other instruments in African cultures, the harp is imbued with special meanings that vary among the different cultures.

Most often, the harp is played by special members of the community, usually men known as *jali* or *griots,* who have been trained since childhood to learn and repeat lengthy oral traditions that relate not only to the people within the group but of the spirit world as well. They keep alive the cultural history and genealogy, using fables and stories from the past to help direct the activities of everyday life.

Lutes/Fiddles

(Because many instruments in this category are played with a bow, instructions are included in the back of this section for making bows.)

Lutes are composed of a sound box or resonating chamber securely attached to one end of a solid neck, with strings that run from one edge of the sound box, across the surface, and along the full length of the neck. The most common method of adjusting tension of the string, or the pitch, is by turning a tuning peg or ring at the far end of the neck. By stopping the string with fingers or a length of metal along the neck, the string length is effectively adjusted, producing another means of pitch adjustment as the instrument is played. Strings may be either plucked or bowed. Traditionally, if the strings are plucked the instrument is classified as a type of lute; if they are bowed, it is considered a fiddle or part of the very large viol family.

Within this category are many different styles of instruments. Important variations include:

- shape and size of body or resonating chamber
- relative size of body and neck, and how they are connected
- number of strings

Simple gourd lute *Photo by David Gamble*

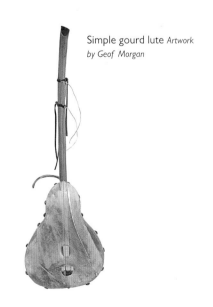

Simple gourd lute *Artwork by Geof Morgan*

Spike Fiddle

Materials

gourd—6–8-inch diameter

dowel—1-inch diameter, 14 inches long

finial, for tuning block

aluminum rod—¼-inch diameter,
   12 inches long

rawhide

glue

decorative edging

leather piece

tuning pegs, handmade or purchased

Tools

saw

sandpaper

stapler

drill

scissors

rat-tail file

rasp

One of the oldest and simplest forms of lute is commonly referred to as the spike fiddle, although the name "pierced fiddle," proposed by Curt Sachs, is more accurate. The feature this class of instruments has in common is a resonating chamber pierced by a slender neck. In many cultures this neck extends out the opposite

Taper the end of the neck so that it fits flush against the gourd body.

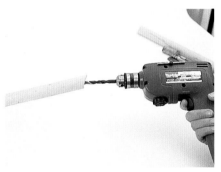

Drill a hole two inches deep and the same diameter as the spike. Drill into the end of the neck at a slight angle where it fits against the gourd.

Glue the metal rod (spike) into the hole drilled into the neck. Find where the rod passes into the gourd so the neck is flush with the top of the gourd, and determine the exit hole on the opposite side of the gourd.

Pull the neck slightly away from the gourd body and put glue around the top of the mouth of the gourd and down the sides for about an inch.

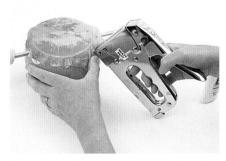

Smooth, stretch, massage, and staple the skin to the top of the gourd body.

Set the staples with a hammer.

Glue a decorative band around the top of the gourd to hide the staples.

Rasp the last two inches of the end of the neck flat for the tuning pegs.

Drill a small hole in the far end of the neck, then rasp the tenon of a decorative finial to fit the hole and glue into place.

Drill two holes through the flattened tuning block. The hole drilled on the top side should be of smaller diameter and drilled first all the way through. Then come back and, from the bottom, drill partly through with a larger drill bit to fit the taper of the tuning peg.

Using a violin peg reamer (or a rat-tail file), ream out the hole until the peg fits snugly.

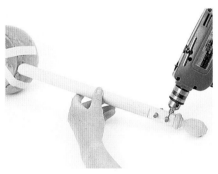

With the pegs inserted into the tuning block, drill a small hole through each peg as close as possible to the tuning block for the string.

Cut two thin sections from scraps for use as a nut and a bridge.

Cut a piece of leather to fit over the spike as a tailpiece. Use it to attach the strings.

The completed spike fiddle and bow *Artwork by Ginger Summit*

side of the chamber and resembles a spike; however, in many other forms the neck extends a short distance, only enough to anchor the strings. When there is a long spike or extension of the neck, the instrument is most often played upright in front of the musician and is rested either on the floor or on the lap or knee. Without a long spike, the instrument is usually held much like a small guitar with the resonator braced against the chest or abdomen.

The correct way to hold the bow for a spike fiddle. Note that, unlike Western bowed instruments, the fingers are placed between the hair and the bow and cause the tension in the bow spring.

"*Olobii Kada*," plucked instrument from northeastern India *Courtesy of Mutua Museum, Manipur Photo by Lai Imo*

"*Tingtila*," bowed instrument from northeastern India *Courtesy of Mutua Museum, Manipur Photo by Lai Imo*

These fiddles usually have one to three strings attached to the short end of the neck and then stretched across the resonator to the upper far end. In the simplest forms, the string is attached to the neck either with a simple knot or a leather ring. Other simple fiddles may have strings attached to tuning pegs. Most have a bridge that rests directly on the membrane and raises the strings from the resonator. In playing the spike fiddle, the string is stopped in midair by being pressed with the fingertip or nail or else by being pinched between the thumb and index finger. It takes a good deal of training to learn to play such an instrument in tune, but once learned, these simple-appearing instruments are very expressive and flexible. This fingering technique works well if the string is bowed, but it is not as effective if the string is plucked.

The variations of this instrument are known by a confusing variety of names, depending not only on the culture or tribe, but on who is allowed to play

Above: Gourd body grown on a mold to achieve the flattened hourglass shape *Photo courtesy of the Palace Museum, Beijing*

Right: Spike fiddle from The Gambia. *Photo by David Gamble*

SOME POPULAR SPIKE FIDDLES

The *inzad* is usually reserved for women musicians in Niger. Among the Tuareg also, only women were allowed to play the *anzad*. Originally it was only played by the wives of warriors, who played the music to protect their husbands with magical powers. Today women play the instrument to accompany male singers. In Mali, the *goge* is played in spirit-possession ceremonies, where it is thought to invoke special powers. The one-string fiddle is also a favored instrument of *griots* or professional musicians in Niger, Nigeria, and Mali. In Ethiopia it is played by musicians who wander from village to village with their "musical newspaper," accompanying themselves as they spread news throughout the countryside.

The *ektar* is a one-string instrument still very popular in India today. It is made with a bamboo stick that passes through a skin-covered gourd. A string is stretched from the bottom end of the bamboo, over a bridge glued to the membrane, and onto a long tuning peg extending through the other end of the stick neck. It is played by holding the neck of the instrument upright in one hand and plucking the string with the index finger of the same hand. In this manner it provides a one-note drone to accompany the singer-musician. With the other hand the musician frequently plays a *kartal* or *sistrum* (rattle) made with metal disks fastened to a wood paddle. Religious mendicants use these instruments today throughout India.

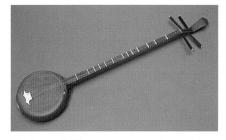

The body of this lute was grown in a mold. Notice the detail in the gourd. *Photo courtesy of the Palace Museum, Beijing*

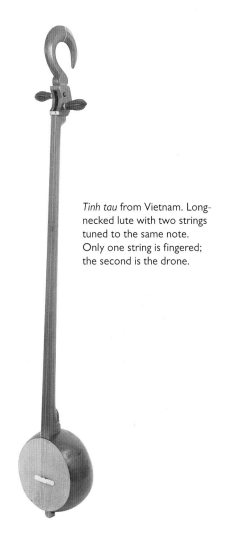

Tinh tau from Vietnam. Long-necked lute with two strings tuned to the same note. Only one string is fingered; the second is the drone.

them and under what circumstances. The significant differences between the instruments are the relative size of the resonator and neck, the materials with which they are made, and the ways in which they are played. Nonetheless, they all retain the basic features of a pierced lute. Because the instrument has such an ancient history, it is no wonder that it has been adapted and modified into so many different forms.

While the spike fiddle appears simple, the music it produces certainly is not. Because it has been used over many centuries and in such different cultural environments, it is only natural that many traditions and taboos surround the instrument, the musicians, and the music. According to Francis Bebee, the musicians of Niger make this simple instrument speak their respective languages with such accuracy that members of one tribe are unable to understand the musical message of a neighboring village.

Several Strings

Lute instruments with more than three strings are the ancestors of the guitar, banjo, or violin family. These instruments are played either flat on the lap or held across the chest in similar fashion to the guitar and lute. The strings are plucked either with the finger or a plectrum made of animal tooth, horn, shell, ivory chip, or metal. Noisemakers or buzzers are frequently attached to the sound box to add additional acoustic interest.

An elaborate form of string lute is the *tambura,* or *tanpura,* one of the most important classical stringed instruments in India. It is most often used as the drone accompaniment for a vocalist, or as part of a musical ensemble including the *veena*

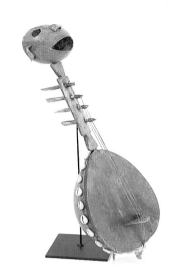

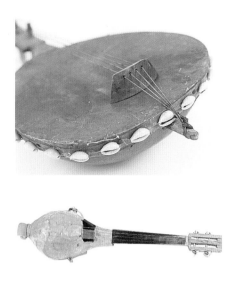

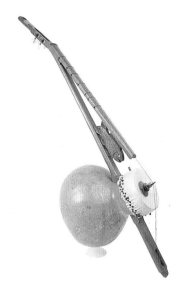

Top: Detail of the African gourd lute

African gourd lute

Bowed gourd lute *Artwork by Geoff Bishop*

Bottom: Gourd guitar *Artwork by Minnie Black*

Gourd banjo *Artwork and photo by Horger Knight*

and *tabla.* It consists of a gourd resonator decoratively attached to a long neck, sometimes up to four and one half feet in overall length. While the resonator traditionally was made of a gourd, today it is frequently carved of tackwood and is completely integrated with the neck. Three wire strings of steel and one of brass are tuned by pegs at the far end of the neck. Occasionally silk thread extends between the wires and the bridge to help give a distinctive buzz to the tone.

Many of our most popular instruments today are derived from these early folk instruments, which were introduced to the Western Hemisphere by both the Europeans and the Africans. Thomas Jefferson reports hearing his slaves play the *banjer,* which he described as one of the most popular instruments of the day. The instrument remained largely an instrument played by Americans of African descent until the early 1800s, when minstrel shows popularized the musical traditions of black slaves. Banjos were made from gourds until the mid-19th century, when other materials began being shaped for the body. A few early settlers in the Southeast continued the tradition of making banjos out of gourds, and that tradition is being maintained to this day by many instrument makers throughout the United States. The distinctive soft sound of the gourd resonator has contributed to the upsurge in popularity.

Making frets

The earliest forms of the lute instrument had one or two strings with a neck made of a round stick or dowel. The string was stopped or pinched by the finger in midair to alter the pitch. However, as more strings were added, the neck was widened to create a flat or slightly curved fingerboard. This allowed the strings to be pressed firmly against the neck to be stopped or shortened. Today, the wider neck can be carved and shaped to pierce the resonator (as in the banjo project), but more frequently the neck is shaped so that it only attaches to one side of the sound box. The strings are anchored either on a wedge that is permanently attached to the soundboard or to a fixture that is mounted on the far side of the resonator. The bottom surface of the neck is sanded and shaped to fit the palm of the hand when the strings are fingered. The wider neck can also accommodate more tuning pegs or the elaborate tuning mechanisms that have been created for guitars.

When a string is pressed against the neck by the soft surface of the finger, some damping occurs and it is also difficult to achieve precise pitches or tones. For this reason, many lutes have frets, or ridges, placed along the neck at specific points. When the string is pressed against the neck, the fret creates a precise terminus for the string, and the pitch is clear and accurate each time it is played. Frets have been made of many kinds of material, including ivory, wood, or metal strips. Some are fastened to the neck in such a way that they can be moved or slid to allow for different tunings, but many are permanently mounted in the fingerboard. Standard frets on contemporary instruments such as guitars and banjos are made of "fret wire," which is commercially available in music stores. It is basically T-shaped, so that the lower portion fits into a slot in the fingerboard and the curved wider portion creates a rigid bridge for the string. The placement of the frets along the neck depends on the tuning desired by the musician, and references for making stringed instruments will provide precise measurements for different tunings. One relatively simple method to gauge this is to use the "rule of 18." The frets are placed so that each shortens the effective string length by ⅟₁₈ relative to the previous fret. There is an easy method for figuring the proper placement:

Measure the distance of the string from the nut to the bridge, which becomes the "vibrating string length," or "VSL." Draw a line this length on a piece of paper. Divide the length by 18, and at one end draw a line that length perpendicular to the baseline. Then draw a diagonal line from the top of the perpendicular line to the far end of the baseline to represent the vibrating string. Using a metal compass, make an arc from the top of the perpendicular line to the baseline; at that point draw another line between the base and diagonal lines. Continue drawing arcs and lines, which identify the placement of the frets along the fingerboard. Note that the frets get closer together as you proceed. Mark these points on the fingerboard for fret placement. You can test the placement by tying a cord around the neck of the instrument at each fret mark. Move these slightly up or down to get the spacing desired, before you permanently mount other frets. (From *Make Mine Music,* by Tom Walther, Little, Brown & Co.)

Gourd double bass *Artwork by Minnie Black*

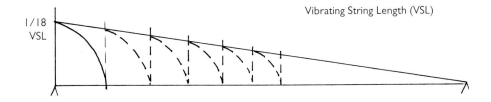

Materials

gourd—10-inch diameter

rawhide

¼-inch dowel, for pegs

glue

banjo neck, carved from a
 block of wood approx.
 3 x 3 inches and 3 feet long

lacing

beads

leather for tailpiece

tuning pegs

strings, nylon

bridge

Tools

saw

sandpaper

rasp

rat-tail file

Banjo with a membrane soundboard

Sand the face of the gourd body perfectly flat.

Using a template, mark on the skin the size of the head and the location of all of the holes for lacing.

Using a template, mark the locations for the holes in the gourd.

Measure down the gourd to mark the exact location of the holes for the pegs.

Drill the peg holes precisely at the marks.

While holding the peg with pliers, put a drop of glue on the end of each peg and insert into the holes.

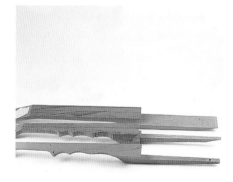

Three stages in carving and shaping the banjo neck from rough cutout to finished neck

Measure the distance between the top of the fingerboard and the top of the spike that will be inserted into the gourd.

Measure down the gourd the same distance to indicate the top of the notch that will be cut into the gourd for the spike.

Cut the notch into the gourd for the spike.

Use a rasp to enlarge the notch just enough to accommodate the spike.

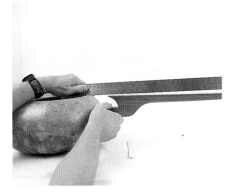

Slide the spike into the notch and check the elevation of the fingerboard to make sure it is level with both sides of the gourd.

While keeping the fingerboard level, mark where the spike touches the opposite side of the gourd by pushing an awl through the wall of the gourd at the center of the spike.

Cut the hole just large enough to accommodate the spike.

Mark and drill a hole in the spike for a locking peg to keep the neck attached to the gourd body of the banjo.

To begin lacing the head (skin), knot a length of rawhide and insert it from inside the gourd through a hole drilled next to the fingerboard.

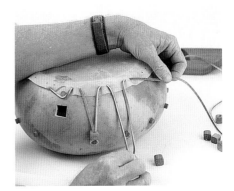

After soaking the rawhide skin until pliable in tepid water, begin lacing the rawhide to the gourd body, making sure a bead is slipped onto a loop of lacing between each peg.

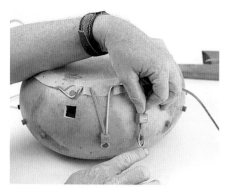

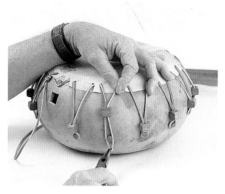

As you tighten the lacing, make sure each loop is brought around its peg and that the bead is next to the peg. Later on, the peg may be pushed up on the lacing to further tighten the head if needed.

Use pliers to help slip the loop of lacing material around the peg and slip the bead down before pulling the lacing tight, then move on to the next loop.

Cut a leather tailpiece that will fit around the spike that emerges from the front of the gourd body. The strings are attached to the tailpiece before they are attached to the tuning pegs.

Ream out the holes in the tuning block so the pegs have a tight fit.

Using a violin peg sharpener, shape the pegs to fit the reamed holes.

Insert and tighten the strings.

Insert the bridge under the strings.

The completed banjo *Artwork by Robert Thornburg*

Robert Thornburg playing his banjo *Artwork by Robert Thornburg*

Guitar with a solid wood soundboard

Materials

dipper gourd, thick shell—24–28 inches long,
    with a large diameter bulb

wood support—1½ x 1½ x 30 inches

wood for fingerboard—¼ x 3 x 24 inches

soundboard—⅛ x 12 x 12-inch plywood

screw (eye screw or finial screw)

tuning pegs, handmade or purchased

Plexiglas, for nut—2 x ½ x ⅛ inches

leather scrap for tail piece

nylon strings

rawhide strip for frets

bridge

Tools

saw

files

sandpaper

drill

glue

masking tape

hobby knife

rat-tail file

After cutting the gourd in half and cleaning it out thoroughly, measure the length for the support piece that will fit the entire length of the gourd.

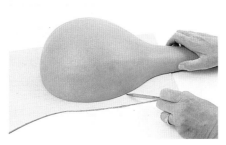

Taper the end of the support piece so it fits flush into the neck of the gourd. The tuning pegs will go through this piece.

Measure the length of the fingerboard.

Trace the profile of the neck of the gourd onto the fingerboard. The fingerboard will extend partway over the soundboard.

Trace the soundboard onto a thin piece of plywood.

Cut out the soundboard and the fingerboard.

Mark where the soundboard fits on the bulb of the gourd.

File, sand, and rasp the edge of the bulb of the gourd to allow the soundboard to fit flush with the top edge of the neck of the gourd. The fingerboard will fit on top of the gourd neck and will overlap the soundboard.

Drill through the gourd into the end of the support rod with a small drill bit. A screw will hold the support rod to the gourd.

Screw a small finial into the drilled hole. The finial will be used to hold the tailpiece, which supports the strings.

Mark and cut out the sound hole in the soundboard.

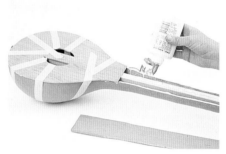

Glue the soundboard to the gourd. Hold in place with masking tape, then glue the fingerboard to the gourd neck and overlap the soundboard.

Sand the soundboard and fingerboard flush with the gourd after the glue has dried.

To remove the wood where the pegs will be, first use the drill.

Then with a hobby knife, cut away the wood between the holes.

Use a rasp or a high-speed drill to finish trimming the two slots.

Mark the placement of the four tuning pegs by temporarily taping them into place on the tuning block. Ideally, the tuning peg will fit completely into the wooden support.

Use an awl to begin the hole at the pencil mark.

Starting with a small drill bit and then gradually using larger bits, drill out the hole for the tuning peg. The hole will need to be tapered so the entry hole will be larger than the hole in the wooden support. Compare your drill bits with the tuning peg to make sure you do not drill a hole larger than the taper.

Use the reamer or the rat-tail file to make the final adjustments to the taper.

Drill a tiny hole through the tuning peg where it will be visible in the slot for the string.

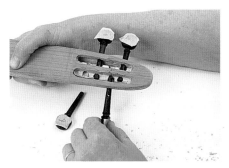

Insert the tuning pegs.

Mark where the nut will attach to the neck.

Saw a shallow slot in the neck for the nut.

Glue the nut into the slot and use a high-speed drill or sandpaper to smooth the edge of the nut.

Cut a leather tailpiece for anchoring the strings.

Make a hole in the end of the tailpiece to slip over the finial at the end of the gourd.

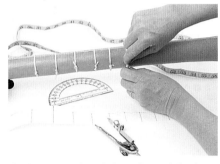

Tie thin strips of rawhide to the neck for frets. Consult the chart in the text to determine the location of each fret.

The completed guitar *Artwork by Ginger Summit Project inspired by Merle Teel*

Gourd violin *Artwork and photo by Fred Bowerman*

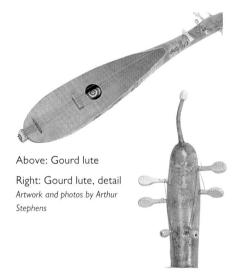

Above: Gourd lute

Right: Gourd lute, detail
Artwork and photos by Arthur Stephens

This fretless guitar is played Hawaiian slack-key style by using an empty CO_2 cartridge as a "bottle neck" to fret the strings. *Artwork by Yvonne Miller*

Making a Bow

Bows are used with stringed instruments to activate the string and create a continuous vibration. Traditionally, horsehair is used for the bowstrings in this country, but in other countries the strings have been made of many other materials, such as gut, plant fibers, and silk. Animal hairs vary in level of coarseness and will create different vibration patterns as they activate the strings. Musicians frequently try to match the hairs, or the composition, of the bow with the strings of the instrument.

Rosin is rubbed on the bowstrings to create the necessary friction as the bow is drawn across the instrument, causing the strings to vibrate.

The simplest bow to make is similar to a musical bow. The stick or piece of wood can be any wood that has a slight give to it (such as ash). Notch both ends of the bow. Make a bundle of approximately 30 horsehairs slightly longer than the piece of wood and put a knot in one end. Soak the bow for about 30 minutes to make it pliable. Slip the knot into the notch at one end of the bow and pull the other ends through the second notch, causing the bow to bend. When you have a sufficient arch in the stick, tie a knot in the other end of the horsehair. When the bow is completely dry, treat the hairs with rosin by holding the block in one hand and drawing the bow back and forth across it firmly.

Another simple way to construct a bow is to use a rigid piece of wood, such

Materials	Tools
dowel—½ x 18 inches	saw
dowel—³⁄₁₆ x 4 inches	drill
2 blocks of wood—	file
1 x ½ x ¾ inch	glue
string—horsehair, thread,	
or monofilament	

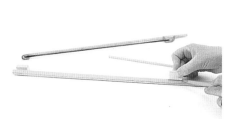
Mark where the blocks will lie on the bow.

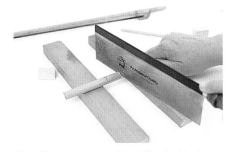
Cut a flat notch in the dowel for the blocks.

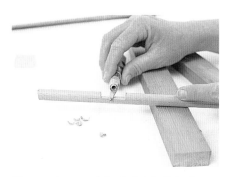
Carve and rasp a perfectly flat shelf for the block.

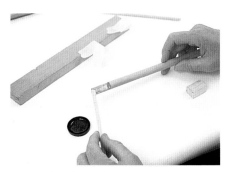
Apply a fast-drying glue to the shelf on the bow.

Glue the blocks into position. They should fit tightly.

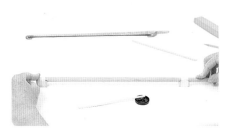
Before the glue has set, turn the bow over and rest it on the blocks to make sure they are aligned. Apply a little pressure to make a tight glue join.

Take a piece of wood that is longer than the distance between the two blocks and put a needle into each end. Wrap thin monofilament or unwaxed polyester cord around the needles, keeping the strands flat and next to each other instead of jumbled. Tie each end into a knot.

Drill a small hole partway into the block on the end of the bow. Put one end of the knotted string into the hole and tap a plug into the hole to secure the end of the string.

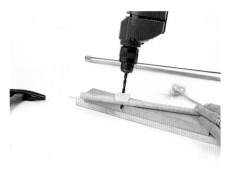

Drill a small hole all the way through the second block partway down the bow.

Pull the knot and remainder of the string through the hole and, while maintaining the tension, flatten and straighten all the strands.

While maintaining the tension, tap in the second plug to hold the strings tight. Trim the knotted strings on the top side of the bow.
Artwork by Ginger Summit

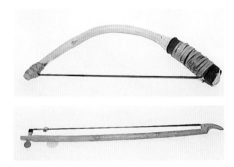

Bows *Photos by Ginger Summit From the collection of San Francisco State College*

as a dowel. Attach blocks of wood on each end and secure the strings with pegs in holes drilled into the blocks. This type of construction allows for some adjustment of the strings if the tension becomes loose.

Zithers

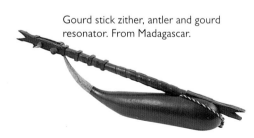

Gourd stick zither, antler and gourd resonator. From Madagascar.

Zithers are instruments with strings that run the entire length of the instrument body and parallel to it. Either the body alone can act as a sound box, or additional resonators such as gourds can be added to enhance the volume. The zither can either be rested temporarily on top of the gourd, or the gourd can be attached to the instrument permanently. In more recent times, the resonator box has been combined with the frame that holds the strings. Hammered dulcimers and autoharps are examples of these instruments. Several simple variations of the zither are common in Africa, and very elaborate forms are identified with music in India and throughout Southeast Asia and the Far East.

Above: *Goong* played by Phong Nguyen. Thirteen-stringed tube zither from Vietnam. *Photo by Phong Nguyen*

Left: *Bro*, a two-stringed instrument played by the mountain people of Vietnam. Carved wood with knob frets. *Photo by Phong Nguyen*

Tube Zither

The tube zither is perhaps the earliest form of this instrument and is still played in many countries today. It is constructed with a single hollow tubular body with the strings extending its entire length. A resonator, very often a gourd, is combined with the tube in some way to amplify the sounds.

One very popular example is found in Melanesia, where strips are cut along the skin of a sago palm tube or a bamboo. The skin is raised from the tube with a bridge, and when dry, the string is plucked or bowed. It is held against either the mouth or a gourd to amplify the sounds.

A very different style of tube zither is the *lokanga voatavo,* found in Madagascar. It is made by stretching a number of strings along a stick. The strings are held under tension by a bridge that is wedged under each one. Rather than having the resonator permanently attached to the stick, one end of the stick is inserted into an opened calabash as the instrument is played. The stick is elaborately carved, and is used to accompany singers or in ensemble with other instruments.

Stick Zither

There are many variations of the stick or bow zither. Some are similar in construction to a musical bow, except the stick is straight rather than arched, with one or more gourds permanently attached to the underside of the stick. Because the frame is rigid, frets are frequently carved or attached to the upper

The deep-pitched *ligombo* trough zither. The Hehe people of Tanzania play this to accompany historical and other songs. Length: 45 inches. *Photo by fine arts students, Rhodes University From the collection of the International Library of African Music, Rhodes University, Grahamstown, South Africa*

surface so the string can produce several pitches. As the instrument is played, the gourd is pulsed against the chest as a variable resonator. Occasionally there is an additional string along the side of the bar, which can be plucked as a drone accompaniment.

Several variations of this instrument are found along the southeast coast of Africa and Madagascar. The wood stick may be carved in several styles, and it may have more than one string. The *herrauou* has three strings, with one producing a drone while the other two strings are used for melody. Other stick zithers are found in many southeastern cultures. The *satiev* of the Khmer people of Kampuchea has a stick body carved of hardwood with a single steel string stretched along its length. A resonator of a half gourd is attached to the stick, and held against the chest as the instrument is played at social occasions such as weddings and during some religious ceremonies.

The *dan bau* consists of a long hardwood wooden frame in which at one end is inserted a flexible bamboo pole one foot high with a gourd attached at its center. A wire string is stretched from the bamboo handle, through the gourd, and firmly attached to the far end of the wooden frame. The instrument is played by stopping and plucking the string with one hand, while the other hand moves the upright bamboo post, changing the pitch by increasing tension on the string. This instrument was originally played by blind street musicians, but now is one of the very popular instruments in Vietnam.

Raft Zither

Many stick or tube zithers can be put together to form what is known as a raft zither. A good example using a gourd as a resonator box is the *toba,* by the Mahi in Dahomey. This instrument is created by first making a raft of reeds, bamboo, millet, or cane. Slits are made in the skin of each tube, so that a thin string is freed from the

The *bangwe* zither of the Sena people of central Mozambique. One string is stretched end-to-end 12 times. The calabash has a 10-inch diameter. *Photo by fine arts students, Rhodes University From the collection of the International Library of African Music, Rhodes University, Grahamstown, South Africa*

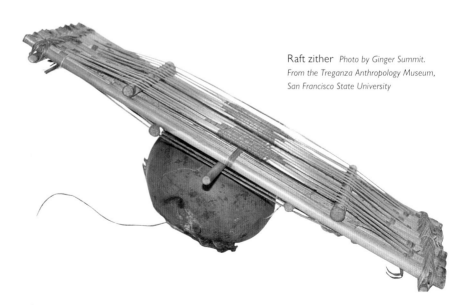

Raft zither *Photo by Ginger Summit. From the Treganza Anthropology Museum, San Francisco State University*

body and allowed to dry. The tubes are then bound together in a raft, and two bridges are wedged between the tubes and the freed skin strings at either end of the raft. The strings are often reinforced by wrapping the entire length with cane or raffia. The wrapping not only strengthens the strings, but can also modify the tone by thickening the vibrating string. The tension and length of the string can also be modified by further wrapping the string to the tube at either end of the raft. The entire raft then rests on an open gourd that amplifies the sounds. The instrument is played by holding the gourd and raft with the fingers and plucking the strings with the thumbs.

Dulcimer

Another very different form of zither is the hammered dulcimer, which is very popular in the United States, particularly in the Appalachian region. This instrument has a single trapezoid-shaped sounding box or resonator that is usually covered with a rigid surface such as a thin piece of wood. Strings extending from one end of the sound box to the other are slightly elevated by bridges at either end. Each string is individually tuned by a peg at one end of the instrument. Occasionally, a gourd is used as the sound box for this instrument. The instrument is played by holding it flat on the lap or other surface and either plucking the strings with fingers or pick, or hammering them with a pair of small sticks or mallets. The autoharp, while not usually constructed with a gourd, is another popular Appalachian zither.

Gourd dulcimer *Artwork and photo by Ethel Owen*

Top left: Gourd dulcimer with five tobacco-box gourd resonators *Artwork by Sue Westhues*

Bottom left: Single snake gourd resonator *Artwork by Sue Westhues*

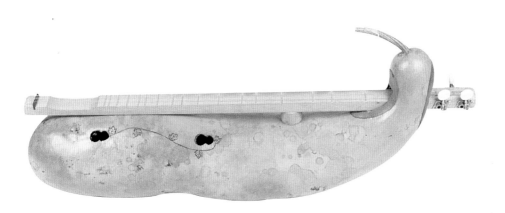

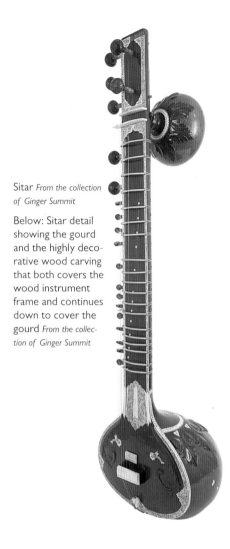

Sitar *From the collection of Ginger Summit*

Below: Sitar detail showing the gourd and the highly decorative wood carving that both covers the wood instrument frame and continues down to cover the gourd *From the collection of Ginger Summit*

An original design using readily available four-inch-diameter PVC pipe for the neck of the *tambura*. The wide, slightly curved bridge provides the buzzing-string drone typical to much of Indian music. The *tambura* is six feet long and 18 inches high. *Artwork by Tony Pizzo Photo by Fletcher Manley*

Veena Family

An elaborate family of zithers evolved in India centuries ago. The *veena* is the instrument of the goddess Saraswatum who, in Hindi mythology, is the goddess of music and who also represents the divine source of wisdom and sound.

The *veena* family of instruments probably evolved a complex interaction of lute-type instruments with the indigenous stick zither. Originally it consisted of a gut string attached to a stick at either end, with two bridges raising the string from the stick.

"*Veena*" is the name of a rather large family of instruments. The *rudra* and *saraswati veenas* are more familiar in southern India, and the *bin* is found in the Hindustani or northern parts of India. (The term "*bin*" is somewhat confusing since it is also occasionally used to refer to a class of aerophones. By far the most common use of the term is in a form of *veena* found in northern India.) They have become very elaborate through the centuries, but certain characteristics remain constant. The strings were originally gut, but now are most often brass or bronze. There are usually seven strings—four to play the melody and three that play drone. The melody strings are stretched across a bridge and frets, and the drones extend along the side of the tube or fingerboard. Sometimes as many as nine to 14 additional strings are passed under the arched frets to create sympathetic vibrations as the upper strings are played.

The sitar combines features of the lute and the zither, and underwent many changes before reaching its present form in the late 18th and 19th centuries. Originally it had three strings and 14 frets. (The name "sitar" derives from the Persian word *tar,* meaning string. *Si-tar* refers to three strings, and although more strings were added at a later date, the name remained.) Through the centuries more strings have been added, so that now the sitar has seven strings that are stretched across a single bridge and 20 movable curved brass frets along the fingerboard. The double sitar also has 11 sympathetic strings extending the length of the fingerboard under the frets. When playing the sitar, only one string is actually fingered to create a melody. The remainder of the strings provide either drone or sympathetic vibrations. The sitar retains the smaller secondary resonator gourd at the top of the fingerboard, which occasionally is removed.

There are several forms of the sitar. In northern India, the term "sitar" is reserved for the instrument with two resonators. *Subahar* (or *swarbahar*) refers to the form that has an enlarged lower resonator and no second gourd on the fingerboard. The *subahar* generally has a lower pitch, up to an octave lower than the sitar, and is played at a slower tempo.

A third related instrument is the *tambura,* which frequently accompanies the sitar and provides the drone accompaniment. The *tambura* is actually a lute instrument, and is discussed further in the section on lutes.

The *veena, bin*, and sitar are large instruments, up to 48 inches in length. There are two main techniques used to play them. The instrument can be placed on the floor in front of the musician, and the strings plucked, much as a zither. The more usual method of holding the instrument is across the chest, with the upper gourd resonator resting on the shoulder. The strings are stopped with the left-hand fingers, and the wrist of the right hand rests on the lower gourd as the fingers pluck the melody.

A single line of melody is plucked with a wire plectrum worn on the finger. A drone note usually accompanies the melody line, played by the small fingers of either hand. If the drone string is not played on the same instrument, a second instrument such as a *tambour* will provide it.

Music in India is based on well-established rhythmic and melodic principles. The rhythms are formalized in the talas, and the melodic patterns are defined by the ragas. Both of these music conventions are rigidly defined by traditions and rules, which vary slightly, depending on the region of India, but they are well known by everyone in the community. Music is based on improvisation within these narrowly defined parameters.

Rudra vina Artwork and photo by Matt Finstrom

Unusual Instruments

There are several unusual instruments that can roughly be classified as chordophones but are difficult to place in one of the other categories. One such instrument is the *gopichand* or *gopiyantra* (also called *khamak, anandolohori,* and occasionally *ektara*). This instrument is found primarily in the eastern region of Bengal, in India. It is a one-stringed drone instrument made from a calabash and large tube of bamboo. The bamboo is split down the middle, with the node at one end remaining intact. The two "legs" created by the split are attached to the sides of the gourd, which has a membrane covering the bottom end. The string is inserted into a hole in the center of the membrane (with the end wrapped around a twig or small stick to keep it in place). The string or wire is

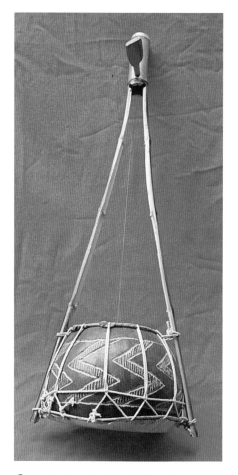

Gopiyantra Artwork and photo by Alberto Magnin

The *gopiyantra* is held in one hand and the finger of that hand plucks the string while that hand squeezes the bamboo together to change the pitch. *Artwork by Ginger Summit*

then stretched from the membrane, through the gourd to the top of the section of bamboo. The string can be mounted for tuning by securing it to a peg inserted through the bamboo. A secondary tuning device is created by a loop of string that is slipped down, encircling the legs of the bamboo. The loop can be slid up or down to create greater tension on the string by squeezing the slats together. To play, the instrument is held in one hand as the string is plucked by the index finger of the same hand. A second method of playing the instrument is to squeeze the bamboo legs with the hand as the index finger plucks the string. By increasing or releasing tension, the tone is bent. The *gopiyantra* is played more by folk singers in northern India and Bengal.

A variation of the *gopiyantra* is the *gubgubbi*. This simple folk instrument is very much like a *cuica,* described in the section on membranophones. It consists of a small drum made with a gourd and with a long string attached to the center of the membrane and passed through the gourd frame. The player holds the

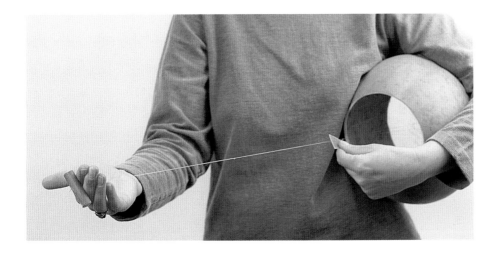

Left: The *gubgubbi* is similar to the *gopiyantra* except that the *gubgubbi* has two holes in the membrane. A doubled string is strung through both holes and tied to a wooden handle or another small gourd. The *gubgubbi* is played by stretching the string with the right hand and plucking the string with the left. The gourd is held under the left armpit. Pitch is changed by pulling on the handle and stretching the string. *Artwork by Ginger Summit*

instrument between his chest and the elbow of the left arm. The right arm holds a knob at the end of the gut string, keeping it taut as the string is plucked with the left hand. Various tones are created by alternately releasing and tightening the string. This instrument is most often used by itinerant musicians in Bengal.

Cut off the top of the bamboo just above the segment. *Artwork by Ginger Summit*

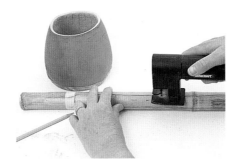

About six inches below the top, begin cutting down the length of the bamboo stalk. Make another cut ¾ inch away and parallel to the first cut. Make the same cuts on the opposite side, to result in two legs attached to the top.

Sand-rasp-file the inside of the legs until they are smooth and flat or almost flat.

With an awl, make three holes in each leg, through the gourd. Stitch each securely to the resonator, keeping the gourd centered.

Taper ¾ of a ¼-inch wooden dowel. Glue a bead to the untapered end for a tuning peg.

Slip wire string through a tiny hole in the skin membrane and up to the tuning peg. Anchor the string below the skin with a bead. Tighten the string with the tuning peg.

Part 4

Aerophones

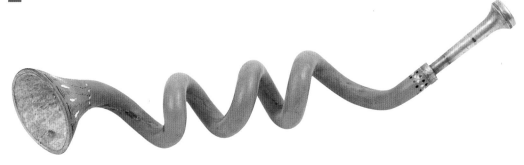

Sound is created by the regular vibration of air molecules. In all of the other categories of instrument described so far in this book, this air vibration is initiated by the movement of a physical object. For example, idiophones are grouped together because air is set in motion by the striking of the rigid body of the instrument; the sound from membranophones is created by the striking of a stretched membrane; and chordophones, by the vibration of a string under tension. In the instruments grouped together as aerophones, the air is first set in motion, usually by blowing, which then hits an edge or other surface, thereby creating a turbulence. The instrument body then selectively reinforces some of the wavelengths that have been produced, thus creating an audible tone or basic pitch. Remember that the enclosed body of air has a natural vibration, just as a solid object does, so it will effectively produce a fundamental as well as distinctive overtones or harmonics.

For most familiar aerophones, the body of the instrument is a tube that can have many shapes—long, short, straight, or very curved. But the bodies can also have other forms, rounded and jug-shaped. By changing the dimensions of the container, it is possible to change or alter the pitch.

Types

Aerophones are subclassified according to how the air is caused to vibrate, or the air turbulence is created, rather than according to the shape of the body. These subclassifications are:

• Sound modifiers: This group of containers may not be considered by many to be instruments, but they are used to modify sounds in many different ways, such as by increasing or muting the volume.

- Flutes: The airstream is directed against or across the sharp edge of a blow hole, thereby creating an "edge tone." When the airstream is blown at the correct angle, about 50 percent of the air is directed above the edge, or outer rim, of the vessel, and 50 percent is directed into the container. This turbulent air is then reinforced, amplified, and shaped by the internal dimensions and other characteristics of the instrument. The hole can be located on the side or on the end of the container. This category includes all manner of flutes and whistles.

- Horns and trumpets: The air is blown between tightly pursed lips, which create a vibration by allowing air to pass in a rapid series of pulses. These instruments have mouthpieces, either integral or detachable, to support the lips as the musician blows into the end of the instrument.

- Reeds: Thin single or double reeds are caused to vibrate by a stream of air. As in lip-buzzed horns, air passes in a series of rapid pulses. The musician blows against, between, or around the reed located in a mouthpiece at the top or front of the instrument. Or reeds may be located on the side of one or more tubes that are inserted into a windchest, chamber, or bladder. When the musician blows into this chamber, the movement of air as it enters the tubes activates the reeds.

- Aeolian: This group of instruments may use elements of the above groups to create the tone, but the airstream in generated by a wind stream, as opposed to a breath of air.

- There are also aeolian aerophones that do not have enclosed bodies of air, but instead activate vibrations in the air that surrounds them. These objects create sound by spinning rapidly, thereby disturbing the air immediately surrounding them and creating sound waves. These are among the most ancient of instruments—the bull roarer and the buzzing disk. Because these two instruments create a general turbulence in the air that is not modified by a resonating chamber, the sound created is heard as noise, often described as wailing or roaring.

Throughout the ages and on every continent, gourds have been used in the construction of instruments in each of these categories. Today many other materials are substituted for the gourd, although in a few areas gourd aerophones are still being made and played.

Basic Principles

Remember some basic principles as you begin planning your aerophone project.

Keep in mind that tones are created by vibrating air. Enclosed columns of air have natural resonating frequencies, and the enclosed cavity will resonate only selected frequencies. Pitch is determined by the length of the vibrating sound wave, and it is the length of the enclosure that establishes the length of the vibrating air column and thus the fundamental pitch. If the column of air (i.e., the tube) is lengthened or shortened, the pitch is lowered or raised. The dimensions of an individual tube or vessel can be altered in several ways.

- A tube can actually be cut to make it shorter (or pieces can be added on, as in some dramatic African horns), which makes a permanent change in the pitch. In order to play different notes, many vessels or tubes of different lengths or volume have to be lined up, as in the pan pipe.
- Holes can be made in the side of the tube, which can be left open or can be plugged by a finger or by keys as the instrument is being played, thereby allowing the single instrument to play many different notes.

The diameter of the vessel or tube and its overall shape, as well as the length, are important, because they emphasize different overtones. The ratio of the length of tube to its diameter will determine the tone quality, or timbre. Shorter, fatter columns have fewer overtones than longer, thinner ones. A round vessel produces different overtones from a tube. A single frequency will be more dominant, and the tone will have fewer overtones and harmonics. Round vessels are often used to make ocarinas, which use a fipple mouthpiece, or vessel flutes, in which air is blown across the notched or sharpened edge of a container.

The principles to remember when using a round-shaped vessel:

- the larger the volume, the lower the pitch
- the smaller the opening, the lower the pitch
- the taller the opening (the longer the neck of the container), the lower the pitch

Tone holes can be used to vary the pitch with round vessels as with other types of aerophones. Hole location is relatively unimportant, unlike hole placement in tube-style containers. The size of the hole is the critical factor with vessel flutes.

The force with which air is blown into the hole will also affect the sound quality as well as the pitch, particularly in tubular-shaped instruments: more will create harmonics or secondary vibrations—readily recognized by the beginner, who produces squeaks and squawks before finding the volume of air that will cause air to vibrate correctly. Overblowing is often used as a technique to produce notes in a higher register.

The material of the instrument greatly affects the harmonics or tone color. Because the insides of gourds are naturally porous, some of the sound waves are absorbed and the tone produced may be soft or weak. For a clear, resonant sound, gourds should be cleaned out and sanded smooth. The inside can also be coated with resin or varnish to further seal the surface, and thereby reflect rather than absorb the sound.

Hollerin' across the "haller" *Artwork by Ginger Summit*

A gourd mute for a trumpet *Artwork by Ginger Summit*

Both apertures of the gourd *udu* drum are played, creating a variety of pitches by bringing the palm down quickly and fully onto the aperture. The sudden air compression makes the sound. *Artwork and photo by Matt Finstrom*

Sound Modifiers

Megaphone

An example of the simplest and most direct use of a gourd as an aerophone is found in the Museum of Appalachia in Tennessee. In many homesteads located in the northern Smoky Mountains, long, tapered gourds were used as megaphones to carry alarms or messages across the hollows. By yelling into the narrow opening, the sounds of the message are concentrated in one direction, effectively amplifying them.

Mute

Musicians today occasionally use a gourd for just the opposite effect—to act as a horn mute. Although they are generally made of plastic, metal, wood, or fiberboard, mutes made from gourds offer special advantages. The spongy inner shell absorbs some of the vibrations and creates a softer, mellower tone than mutes made of other materials.

Plosive Aerophone

The "plosive aerophone," or percussion pot, includes instruments commonly referred to as drums: the pottery drum or *udu* in Nigeria, *dilo* or *ghagar* in Pakistan, and *ghatam* in India. Traditionally, they are clay pots with a relatively narrow neck opening on top, very similar in shape to a bottle gourd. They are played by slapping the flat of the hand or a broad mallet over the opening, thereby causing a rush of air into the vessel, which creates a low tone. The other hand often beats a rhythm on the side of the container as well. Occasionally there is a hole on the side of the vessel that is either left open or is covered with a membrane; this is manipulated with the other hand to create a pulsing distortion of the tone.

While these instruments are similar in shape and usage to the *ipu* found in Hawaii, the main difference between them is the way in which they are sounded. Because the *ipu* is slapped on the side or bottom of the gourd, it is classified as an idiophone—the vibration is initiated by hitting the rigid surface of the instrument. With the percussion pot, the initial vibration is created by slapping the top, which forces a turbulent airstream into the container, amplifying the sound, thus qualifying it as an aerophone.

By using a gourd that is thoroughly cleaned and sealed, you can create a percussion drum that will sound similar to the traditional *udu*.

Flutes

Flutes encompass a broad range of aerophones, not simply the familiar orchestral instrument. The feature that all of them have in common is that an airstream is directed against a sharp edge or rim of a blowhole, which divides the airstream,

Each of the eight vessel flutes plays one note of the scale. *Artwork by Ginger Summit*

breaking it into smaller disturbances or vibrations. The airstream can be blown through an opening in the side of the body or through one open end. The end may be completely open with one sharp edge or may have a fipple mouthpiece, similar to a recorder or pennywhistle. The body can be a familiar tubular shape or can be rounded or globular, like an ocarina.

Flutes have been found on every continent, and examples exist from the Stone Age. Ancient flutes were made of materials such as bone, cane, bamboo, or other wood. The few remaining preserved gourd aerophones are vessel flutes, with round bodies.

Simple Vessel Flutes

Simple one-note instruments can be made by cutting off the top of a bottle gourd, cleaning it thoroughly, and blowing across the top. Use several different sizes and shapes of gourds to create a whole collection of different notes. (Remember, it is the volume of air, not the shape, that will determine pitch.) These can be played by several people to create a melody of sorts. With each player taking a turn blowing into a gourd at the correct time, many people can produce simple tunes.

The vessel flute is played by blowing across the opening so that breath hits the sharp edge on the opposite side. *Artwork by Xavier Quijas Yxayotl*

Making a vessel flute

One of the challenges to making a vessel flute is to clean the interior thoroughly. First cut off the top and scrape out as much pulp and seeds as possible with a skewer or other bent wire. If pulp remains on the inside, soak the gourd for several days. Add rough-edged gravel and shake vigorously to loosen the remaining bits. Pour out, and repeat the process until the interior is completely clean and smooth. You may also want to coat the inside of the vessel with varnish or polyurethane to seal the pores.

You can adjust the note, or pitch, of the gourd vessel by increasing or decreasing the inside volume or by altering the opening at the top. Cut or trim the opening of the gourd to make a permanent change, or add water or small gravel for a temporary reduction in the interior volume to create a slightly higher pitch.

Vessel flute *Artwork by Darrel Devore*

Examples

The Chickahominy and Panunkey natives of the southeastern United States made small gourd whistles by cutting across the neck of a small pear-shaped gourd and boring two pairs of holes on one side. Water inside the gourd

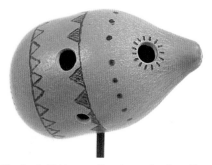

The *ipu hokiokio* nose flute is usually played by being held under the right nostril, with the thumb closing the left nostril and the fingers of the left hand opening and closing the tone holes. *Artwork by B. Ka'imiloa Chrisman, M.D.*

The *ipu hokiokio* is played with the nose. *Artwork and photo by B. Ka'imiloa Chrisman. M.D.*

modified the pitch. The whistle or "blow gourd" was used for songs and entertainment much as an ocarina or harmonica is used today. Hunters used a similar whistle without holes to signal other Indians in the area; a single sharp note let them know each other's whereabouts in a swamp or forest, and two notes indicated "SOS," or "Come quickly."

Gourd whistles in Hawaii, called the *ipu hokiokio,* are played with the nose. They are also small and pear-shaped, ranging in size from two to four inches in length and diameter. These whistles with two or three note-producing holes were designed to be blown either from the end or from the side. They are called "lovers' whistles," as they were often used during courtship.

Actually, nose flutes have been found in all five continents and in many forms, including vessel and tube shapes. According to Curt Sachs, nose breath was considered far more potent than mouth breath, and thus more closely connected to the soul. These instruments were usually associated with magic and religious rites.

Tube Flutes

The more familiar shape of a flute is tubular. Tube flutes are made of many different kinds of materials, such as hollowed branches, grasses, bone, metal, and even plastic. The handles of dipper gourds make an excellent tube for a flute if they are cleaned sufficiently. Sound is created in a flute by blowing across or against a sharp edge, which divides the airstream, thus creating a turbulence within the instrument body. Following are several techniques for making a gourd flute.

Simple edge-blown flutes

The simplest form of edge-blown flute requires the musician to blow across an opening in the tube. While these flutes are relatively easy to make, they require great practice and skill to direct the airstream in precisely the right angle to produce a good tone. These instruments have been popular throughout history around the world, and remain a familiar instrument today in many cultures.

End-blown

To make an end-blown flute, select a dipper gourd with a narrow neck. A flute can be of any length, but should be approximately one-half to one inch in internal diameter. The longer the tube, the lower the initial fundamental and the greater the number of notes that can be produced. A one-note whistle can be made of a tube as short as three inches. For a flute with three to four notes, select a gourd with a neck about 12 inches.

Cut the tube handle off a dipper gourd, with openings on both ends, and clean thoroughly. On one side of the opening at the stem end, shape a notch or a rounded dip. Carefully sand or file this area to create a sharp edge, sloping down to the outside of the gourd. Strengthen this surface by rubbing it with varnish or glue. Sand the edges of the gourd so that it is smooth when held against the lips, or put beeswax on the edges except for the notch with the sharp edge. To play, hold the edge against the lower lip and blow carefully, directing the airstream across the sharpened edge or notch on the opposite side. Adjust the stream of air until a fundamental tone is sounded. Holes can be made in the sides of the tube to make additional notes. Examples of this type of instrument are the Japanese *shakuhachi* and the Middle Eastern *ney*. Often the bottoms of these tubes are closed, which essentially turns them into vessel flutes. The pan pipe is a row of these tubes fastened together so that one instrument can produce several notes.

Transverse flutes

The side-blown flute is what most people associate with the term "flute." It is a tube of 12 to 18 inches in length that is plugged at one end. The musician directs the airstream across a hole in the side near the plug and adjusts the tone by covering other holes in the side of the tube. This type of instrument continues to be popular throughout the world today. Although it is easy to make, experimentation and practice are necessary to find the proper orientation of the airstream.

The gourd amplifies the membrane attached to the flute. *Artwork by Romey Benton*

1. To make the flute, select a dipper gourd with a handle at least 12 to 16 inches long. You may want to leave a flare on the end, but do not count the flare as you measure the length of the tube.
2. Even though the end nearest the blowhole is naturally plugged by the stem end, cut the end off and replug it with a dowel or cork. The distance from the stopper to the center of the blowhole is important to tone quality. The best tone will be produced when the distance roughly equals the internal diameter of the tube. A cork or dowel will permit more control over this dimension.
3. Cut a ⅜-inch blowhole one inch from the end of the tube. With sandpaper, smooth the edges, rounding them slightly on the inside of the shell. File the hole so it is slightly more oval than round.

    Test the tone of the flute by blowing into it before drilling any finger holes. Move the end plug slightly to adjust the fundamental pitch, or cut the overall length of the pipe to make it shorter and therefore raise the pitch.
4. See pp. 117 for guidelines on the placement of the fingerholes.

Materials	Tools
dipper gourd 12–16 inches long	saw
cork or dowel, to fit interior of gourd	hobby knife
neck	tape measure
varnish	sandpaper
	round file

The larger dipper gourd case holds the smaller dipper gourd flute. *Artwork by Robert Hilton*

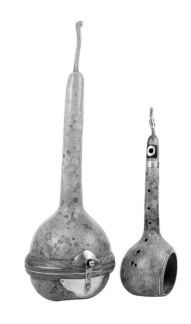

Duct flutes

A recorder is an example of an end-blown flute with a fipple mouthpiece, which directs the airstream through a duct against a sharp edge of a blowhole cut in the side of the gourd. This type of opening is frequently found on whistles of all shapes and sizes. If the mouthpiece is properly aligned, it is easy to direct the airstream against the edge and create a reliable sound. A fipple mouthpiece is tricky to make, but is much easier to play than the other types of flutes since the airstream is automatically aimed at the sharp edge.

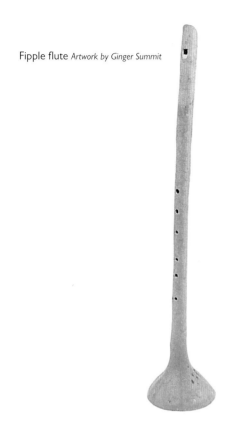

Fipple flute *Artwork by Ginger Summit*

Airstream

Recorder-type flute

1. Cut off both ends of the tube. (A bell flare can be left on the bulb end by removing only part of the dipper portion of the gourd, but the bell will have minimal effect on the tone. The length of the instrument should be measured from the end of the tube, not the edge of the bell.) The tube can be of any length, from three inches to two feet, depending on the number of notes and the lowest fundamental pitch you wish to create. Remember, it is easy to trim or shorten the length of the tube once the mouthpiece is in place, so don't start with too short a tube.

2. Clean the interior with a wire or bottle brush, and sand as smooth as possible. This can be done by wrapping sandpaper around a sponge that is glued on a long dowel handle or by working steel wool or a copper scrub pad back and forth inside the tube. The smoother the inner wall, the purer the tone. Varnish or seal if desired.

3. Cut a small window in the side of the gourd, approximately one inch from one end, to form the aperture and sharp edge. Begin by making a shallow cut straight into the side of the gourd. Enlarge the hole with a knife by carving carefully toward the cut, thus creating a semicircular opening, the sharp edge facing toward the stem end of the tube. (You can reinforce the sharp edge later by coating it with varnish or glue.)

   The shape of the window will affect the sound. A narrower window creates more overtones. Start by making a small window—it can always be adjusted and enlarged as you experiment with the tone of the instrument.

4. Make a plug that will fit securely into the opening, either of dense cork or wood dowel. It should be approximately one inch long.

5. Flatten one side with a knife, and sandpaper to create an angled surface. This angle will direct the airstream directly to a sharp edge cut in the side of the gourd. You will have to experiment with the angle of this edge. See the drawing.

6. Tap the cork into place.

7. Blow through the windway to check for sound. If you do not get a sound, try adjusting the cork slightly by pushing in or out to change the airstream. Sometimes a piece of plastic placed on top of the slanted surface of the plug helps direct the airstream. If you still do not get a sound, remove the plug and try again with a different slant. Once you get a reliable tone, mark the position of the cork, and glue it in place.

8. To make the fingerholes, follow the suggested measurements in the section on page 117.

Because the overtones are greatly affected by the quality of the material of which the instrument is made, gourd flutes will always have their own unique sounds. You can modify this by coating the interior with resin or several coats of varnish, but the thickness and density of the shell will always have an effect.

Cut off the globe of the dipper gourd, but leave a bell end.

Cut off the stem end.

Fipple Flute

Materials	Tools
dipper gourd neck	saw
cork or dowel, to fit	sandpaper
opening of gourd	hobby knife
neck	short awl or ice pick
varnish	round file

Thoroughly clean out the gourd bell and tube.

Run a dowel up and down the tube to loosen the pith.

Draw a square on the tube beginning about an inch and a half from the end.

Cut out the square, making sure that the farthest edge is angled with a sharp edge facing the blowhole.

Trim a one-inch section of cork to fit the end of the tube.

Sand a 30–45-degree angle on the plug.

Fit the plug into the mouthpiece end.

If the fit is not quite right, cut a piece of thin plastic (from a water bottle) to fit on top of the plug to direct the air to the right position.

Push a plug and/or a plastic shim into place.

Ocarina with external fipple
Artwork by Carolyn Rushton

Ocarina with internal fipple *Photo by Esteban Gonzalez*

Bamboo slot flute with gourd bell, above, and all-gourd flute, below. *Artwork by Cliff Walker*

Ocarina

Ocarinas are round vessel flutes with a fipple mouthpiece. To make these, first make a short fipple mouthpiece using a bit of dipper gourd handle and then attach it to the side of a cleaned gourd. The vessel essentially acts as a resonating chamber for the mouthpiece. If you are having trouble making a fipple mouthpiece, you may want to simply use the mouthpiece of an old recorder or pennywhistle, and attach it to a gourd body.

You can also use a dipper gourd or other small bottle gourd that has a narrow portion at the stem end. Cut, leaving approximately two inches of the stem before the gourd swells into a bulb. In this short section, make a fipple mouthpiece, following the instructions above.

Native American slot flute

A distinctive style of duct flute known as a "slot flute" is used to make the spirit flute most frequently associated with North American Indians. The plug, or slanted surface that directs the airstream, is located several inches from the initial hole into which the player blows. Originally this flute was made of cane, a North American grass of the bamboo family. The slot was placed across the naturally occurring section that plugs the tube. Air blown in one end was directed over the section filament through a slot, then directed back into the tube by way of the sharp edge at the end of the slot.

Fingerholes

Flutes can be made with no fingerholes—which play only one note—while others have as many as eight holes. The tables on the next page give recommended measurements for hole placement. However, gourd dimensions and shell thickness vary tremendously, and it is difficult to predict accurately what placement is best for holes in the gourd selected. Here are some general guidelines that will help in this process:

- Before making any fingerholes in the instrument, finish it to a point that the mouthpiece makes a consistent tone. This will be the lowest pitch that is possible in this vessel or container. Trim the end of the vessel to get the pitch desired as the fundamental.
- One way to determine hole placement is simply to hold the flute comfortably and mark on the tube where your fingers are. Make a small hole at the point farthest from the mouthpiece (at least two inches from the end of the tube). Cover and uncover this hole to hear how it sounds with the fundamental. By making the hole a little larger you can raise the note. You can elongate the hole up or down the tube to slightly raise or lower the note. Continue in this way, adding holes one at a time, until you are able to create several notes.
- For a more accurate placement of holes, you can use the following measurements as a guideline. They were originally intended as suggestions for holes

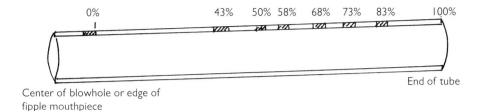

0% 43% 50% 58% 68% 73% 83% 100%

Center of blowhole or edge of
fipple mouthpiece

End of tube

in tubes that are regular and consistent, such as metal or plastic. Because gourds usually have inconsistent interior surfaces and diameters, these measurements should be considered as guidelines only. See the drawing above.

While the holes will eventually be about ⅜ inch, it is better to start with smaller holes and sand them slightly to enlarge and smooth the edges. You can affect the individual notes slightly by modifying the size of the hole. Raise the pitch by enlarging the hole slightly, and lower the pitch by making the hole smaller. It is clearly easier to begin with a smaller hole, and then enlarge it. Don't make the holes too large or your fingertips will not adequately cover them.

Horns

The important distinction between instruments classified as horns and those as flutes is in the way that the air is caused to vibrate. In horns and trumpets, the player's lips are pursed tightly together, and air is blown between them to create a pulsation. By blowing in this way into a resonating chamber, certain frequencies are reinforced, creating tones.

Horns and Trumpets

In musical convention, historically the terms "horn" and "trumpet" were used to refer to instruments that differed in shape but were similar in the way they were played.

In early instruments, both trumpets and horns could be either end-blown or side-blown. On rare occasions carved or wood cups were fitted into the end as a brace for the lips. The term "trumpet" referred to an instrument that had a straight tube that was conical in shape. The term "horn" referred to a tubular instrument that had a consistent diameter throughout its length, which was often curved. In this discussion, the term "horn" will be used to refer to all lip-vibrated aerophones.

Cultural history

Primitive horns are found in every continent, made from a variety of materials, including wood, bamboo, clay, metal, shells, horns, and even tusks. Gourds were used extensively for horns throughout sub-Saharan Africa and Central America, and at least one example of a Maori gourd trumpet has been found in New

Gourd trumpet played with the side of the mouth *Artwork by Guillermo Martinez*

Demonstration of *gbinna* musical instruments, Bodwai, Nigeria *Photo by Marla C. Berns*

Gourd trumpet *Artwork by Bryce Maritano*

Zealand. They have been made in many sizes, from small horns supported by one hand, to large instruments that are supported on the floor or on a special stand. One very unusual style of horn is the *penah,* played in the Sudan. It is made of a bottle gourd, with a blowhole in the bottom round end of the gourd. The neck is cut off, and the opening is plugged by the hand and muted while being played. Three different sizes, ranging from 18 inches to 30 inches in diameter, are played to accompany the lyre for dances and ceremonies.

As is frequently seen with other musical instruments, trumpets and horns were often associated with power, ritual, and mystic ceremonies, and the players were either the political leaders, the shamans, or specially trained musicians. The instruments may have had one or two holes to allow different pitches, but the tones were usually controlled by the lip tension and breathing of the musician. The belief was that the sounds produced magical powers that could scare away evil spirits and protect the tribe. The gourd resonators provided a link between the realms of the living and the dead. For example, they were used in funeral celebrations to awaken ancestral spirits.

Gourds were frequently combined, either with other gourds or with other materials, to make very long resonating chambers. As many as four gourds, joined with a plaster of mud and dung and covered with hide, could be combined to form unusually long trumpets. Horns of four to six feet in length can be found in Nigeria, Tanzania, Uganda, and Cameroon.

The materials most frequently combined to make horns included wood and either hollowed branches or bamboo. These had slightly different shapes and configurations in different tribes.

Instructions for making a horn

In making a gourd horn or trumpet today it is easiest to combine a mouthpiece already designed for a trumpet or other brass instrument with a gourd resonating chamber. Just as horns come in many unusual shapes and sizes, the options for selection of a gourd are very broad. Start with a medium-handled dipper gourd, the stem of which will fit snugly around the mouthpiece. Reinforce the opening of the neck of the gourd by gluing a ring of surgical tubing around the inner edge. This will create a rubbery surface that grabs the mouthpiece firmly and protects the gourd shell from cracking. Wrap the outside of this edge with cord, leather thong, or thin wire for additional reinforcement. By leaving a portion of the bulb end of the gourd you will create a long tube with a bell flare at the end.

To play: Wet your lips and purse them together, as though sounding the let-

The gourd was specially grown for this instrument. The innards are removed by filling the gourd with water and letting the water rot out the membranes. A traditional bugle mouthpiece is used. *Artwork by Bart Hopkin*

ter "m." Open them slightly as you blow, creating a vibration and a buzzing noise. By bracing your lips against the mouthpiece, the airstream is directed into the resonator, where certain harmonics are reinforced. Tighten or relax your lips to get different tones.

Didgeridoo

A *didgeridoo* is an instrument of the Australian aborigines that is traditionally made of a four- to six-foot-long branch that has been hollowed out by termites. It is played by continuously blowing air through pursed lips, using a technique called circular breathing. While the resonating characteristics will be different, it is possible to make this instrument out of the handle of an extra-long handled dipper or a snake gourd that is at least two inches in internal diameter. Clean the gourd thoroughly and seal the inside with a varnish or sealer. The rim that is blown into should be coated with a thick ring of beeswax to form a cushion for the lips.

Musicians have also made *didgeridoos* from hollow bamboo tubes, attaching gourd bells to enhance the tone.

Reeds

A reed instrument is an aerophone that relies on the vibration of reeds to initiate the sound wave (as opposed to being blown between the lips or across a blowhole). A thin, pliable material is placed over an opening in the instrument body. The reed pulses back and forth as the airstream rushes past, causing the vibration that produces the tone. This category received its name because the coverings were made from the stalks of cane, which were both light and springy. Today, most reed instruments still use reeds made from cane, which can be purchased in music supply stores in a wide variety of sizes, shapes, and pliability. However, reeds cut from various weights of plastic, such as refrigerator containers and water or milk jugs, also make a very effective instrument. There are several ways these can be configured over the opening of the air passage. Like horns, most reed instruments have both a mouthpiece and a resonating chamber.

The gourd has been used in the construction of both mouthpiece and resonating body. It is frequently combined with other materials to create an unusual variety of instruments. Bamboo tubes with gourd bodies are probably the most frequent combination, and these instruments are still played in South America, Africa, India, and the Far East.

Making a Single-Reed Mouthpiece

Creating a single-reed mouthpiece is less complicated, and there are three different ways it can be done. An important consideration is the material available for

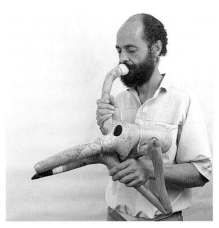

Gourd trumpet *Artwork by Robert Hilton*

Above: Bamboo *didgeridoo* with gourd bell *Artwork by Romey Benton*

Left: Gourd *didgeridoo* made from two snake gourds joined in the middle. It is difficult to find one snake gourd of sufficient length and diameter. *Artwork by Paul Sedgwick*

making the reed. You may purchase a reed that is made for a clarinet or saxophone. These are available in most music stores in various widths. Purchase several, so you can select the width to fit your gourd tube. Many other materials are also suitable, each of which will produce a slightly different tone and timbre: various weights of plastic, thin metal, or even cane. Make several reeds so you can find a tone quality that satisfies you.

Idioglottal reed—"the primitive clarinet"

The oldest type of single-reed opening is an idioglottal reed. This term refers to a flap that is partially sliced from the body of a tube, such as reed cane or millet stalk. It is left attached at one end, so that when air is blown over it, the flap pulses and creates air vibration in the tube. The near end of the tube is sealed and the entire end, including the reed, is placed inside the mouth. Because the gourd shell is not flexible, this type of opening can be approximated by cutting a window in the side of a gourd tube and then covering it with a flap made from another material, such as a plastic milk bottle.

Instructions for making an idioglottal reed

1. Cut a tube of gourd, such as from the handle of a thin dipper. The tube should be ½–¾-inch in diameter, so that you can put it into your mouth comfortably.
2. It is not necessary to remove the stem end of the gourd, since the tip of this mouthpiece is closed. However, it is essential that the tube be completely clean. Sometimes it is hard to remove all the pulp from the base of the stem. In this case, cut off the tip and replug the hole with a cork or wooden dowel.
3. Flatten one side of the tube approximately one-half to one inch from the end by filing or sanding.
4. Cut a narrow window in the flattened area close to the closed end, about ¼–½ inch long.

Top right: Idioglottal reed of cane made by slicing a very thin sliver of skin, which then vibrates when air rushes over it. Compare this to the idioglottal attached to a gourd tube and made from a plastic milk bottle. Rubber bands hold the reed and seal the *pungi*. *Artwork by Ginger Summit*

Bottom right: "A precursor to both clarinets and bagpipes, the *pungi* is a type of double clarinet that has a large gourd as a wind-chamber mouthpiece and usually has one melody and one drone pipe. The reeds are made from the same kind of cane as the pipes and are simply cut into a smaller piece of cane at a nodal point and inserted into the end of the larger piece. It requires circular breathing to create the continuous drone, which on many of these instruments is quite a challenge. (This obviously is why someone invented a bag on the bagpipe to create the continuous flow of air.)"—Randy Raine-Reusch *From the collection of Jane Woolverton*

5. Make a flap of thin, springy plastic (from a milk bottle, for example) that is just large enough to cover the opening. Fasten it over the window by tying or taping one end to the flat part of the gourd tube. Bend the flap slightly upward so it doesn't rest completely over the window. Secure it with string, rubber band, or tape. It doesn't matter which end of the flap is secured to the gourd.

Materials	Tools
neck of dipper gourd	saw
flat piece of plastic	hobby knife
(4 x 4 inches) from	sandpaper
a gallon milk jug	wood rasp
rubber band or	short awl or ice pick
masking tape	round file
waxed linen or string	scissors

Cut the stem off the end of the dipper and make a cut about one quarter inch into the gourd about 1¼ inches from the end.

File, rasp, carve, or sand the shelf flat from the end of the gourd to the cut. Stop just before you rasp completely through the wall of the gourd. Cut a small rectangle into the tube through the shelf.

Sand the shelf perfectly flat.

Cut a rectangle of plastic from a commercial water bottle.

Trim the plastic reed so it just covers the rectangular opening into the gourd, and tape it in place with masking tape just at the far end next to the step up.

Place the end of the dipper, including the entire reed, into your mouth so that your lips are around the gourd tube, and blow. The reed should vibrate and cause a sound. Keep adjusting reed and tape until you hear a reedy tone. That's the fundamental.

While blowing across the reed, lightly run your fingers up and down the tube and feel the vibrations in the tube. Where you feel the strongest vibration, mark the point and make a small hole with your awl. That's the first tone hole.

Enlarge the hole to one quarter of an inch using the end of a riffler rasp or knife. Keep the hole symmetrical and clean.

Continue playing the fundamental by closing off the tone hole and feeling for vibrations for the second, third, and fourth holes, and so on. *Artwork by Ginger Summit*

If the air does not go through the window or causes the flap to seal the opening, bend the flap upward slightly to create more gap between it and the tube. If too much air goes through the opening so that no sound is made, adjust the tie of the flap. You can control the pitch slightly by making small adjustments in where and how the flap is tied and the flap's length. Once you have achieved a consistent tone (which is the fundamental for the length of the pipe), you can make tone holes as described for flutes.

This type of reed mouthpiece is the ancestor of today's clarinet and saxophone, and is still used in the bagpipe and snake charmer's flute.

Pungi

An unusual reed instrument very popular in southern India is used by snake charmers to entrance their cobras. Known both as a *pungi* and *tiktiri*, this instrument consists of two bamboo or cane pipes with idioglottal reeds inserted into the bulb end of a small gourd. (These pipes can also be made of handles of a dipper gourd.) A blowhole is bored into the narrow neck of the gourd wind chamber. Since it would be a mouthful to play both pipes at the same time, the gourd serves as both the mouthpiece and the air cavity, allowing more than one pipe to be blown at the same time. Tone holes are made in the pipes, one of which plays the melody and the other of which acts as a drone. By using circular breathing, the skilled musician is able to produce a continuous tone.

"Most common in India, the *pungi* is used to charm cobra snakes. Cobras when threatened will raise part of their body off the ground and puff out their heads as a warning. Some people think that the cobra is attracted to the sound of the snake charmer, but snakes do not have ears. As the shape of the pipe is similar to that of an erect cobra, the movement of the instrument when played and the shape of the instrument are more likely reasons for the snake's behavior."— Randy Raine-Reusch *Photo by Jane Woolverton*

Pungi Artwork by Pat Wilkinson

Make two pipes of different lengths. Make tone holes in one but not the other. Put a thumb hole on the back side of the second pipe. Cut a hole in the bottom of a larger gourd that will hold the two pipes. Cut the stem end open for a mouthpiece.

Insert the two pipes into the hole of the cleaned-out windchest.

Pungi tubes are sealed with a section of rubber from the inner tube of a tire. *Artwork by Ginger Summit*

Clarinet-type reed mouthpieces

Most clarinet-type instruments have mouthpieces that are precisely molded to create accurate tones, and it is possible to make an instrument and attach the mouthpiece for a saxophone or clarinet to it. However, you can make a reed mouthpiece that roughly approximates these in both shape and tone.

1. Select a dipper handle that has a ½–⅝-inch internal diameter.
2. Cut both ends to create a tube at least one to two feet in length. It is quite appropriate to leave a bell from a dipper gourd at one end. You can even attach a new gourd bell after the instrument has been made. Different shapes and sizes of bell will affect the overtones produced by the tube, so experiment with several and consider making interchangeable bells. Clean the gourd thoroughly inside and out.
3. At the stem end of the gourd, make an angle cut between 20 and 30 degrees. The angle of the cut has some effect on tone quality, so you can adjust the cut as you go along by testing the reed against the cut. Begin by sanding the cut perfectly straight, and then adding a very slight curve at the tip of the

Materials	Tools
neck of dipper gourd	saw
flat piece of plastic	sandpaper
(4 x 4 inches) from	pencil
a gallon milk jug	heavy thread
hobby knife	scissors
waxed linen or	short awl or ice pick

Thoroughly clean out the gourd and the neck.

Sand the cut edge to make it perfectly flat, then sand a slight taper (lay) to the end of the cut.

Place the cut end on a piece of plastic and trace the profile.

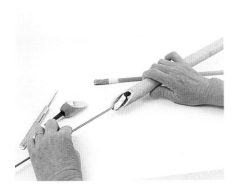

Cut out the plastic reed.

Mark on the side opposite the reed for an anchor for the tie.

Cut a small groove across the neck where the mark is. Tie the plastic reed into place. It should be perfectly flat against the cut edge of the gourd except for a little gap at the near end to allow a little air in to lift the reed.

Playing the gourd saxophone, the lower lip is against the bottom of the reed. Allow the reed to vibrate. This takes much practice.
Artwork by Ginger Summit

Detail of mouthpiece *Artwork by Romey Benton*

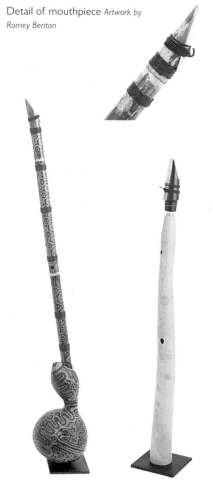

Left: Bamboo clarinet with gourd bell *Artwork by Romey Benton*

Right: All-gourd clarinet with commercial clarinet mouthpiece *Artwork by Romey Benton*

angle (the top quarter of the cut). This angle is called the "lay," and creates a slight gap for the flow of air between the reed and the mouthpiece.

4. To make a reed that completely covers the opening you have made, cut a square of plastic from the flat side of a one-gallon milk jug, of the type found in most supermarkets. Trim the plastic over the opening so it fits the curvature of the end of the tube.

5. Test the mouthpiece by first moistening the reed and then tying, taping, or securing it to the tube with a rubber band. Put your mouth over the mouthpiece so that your lower lip is on the base of the reed and your mouth is tight around the gourd tube. Blow gently.

6. You can make adjustments in the tone by removing the reed and sanding the tube:

- If the reed closes tight against the opening and doesn't allow air to pass, sand more off the top edge of the gourd.
- If too much air goes through the opening and no sound is created, the gap is too large and you need to flatten the surface.
- If the tone created is a pulsing squeal instead of a steady tone, adjust the gap and clean out the edges of the inside of the tube. Keep trying until the mouthpiece produces a nice, even tone as you blow.
- You can alter the pitch by adjusting the attachment of the reed to the tube: 1) press against the reed slightly with your lower lip to create a temporary pitch change; 2) move the cord (or rubber band or tape) that secures the reed back and forth until you are able to get a consistent tone.

Free-Reed Aerophones

The third class of reed aerophone is the free reed. It differs from the other reed instruments in that the reed flap is smaller than the window opening. It is attached to the instrument body at one end, and when activated by an airstream vibrates in and out of the opening (much like a swinging door). This way the sound is created whichever direction the airstream goes, i.e., breathing in or out.

One family of instruments found throughout Southeast Asia, Korea, China, and Japan utilizes this principle. Many bamboo pipes are fitted into a small windchest, which acts as the air reservoir. In China it is known as a *sheng*; in Japan, the *sho*; in Laos and Thailand it is known as a *khaen*; and in Korea as a *saing* (or *saenghwang*).

It has been traced back to southern China, to at least 3000 B.C., based on illustrations in manuscripts and court papers. The oldest intact instrument was found in a treasure storage area along with many other instruments dated from at least 1000 B.C.

The instrument is thought to have originated in the region of Burma or Laos, and from there spread south to Thailand and Borneo, north to China and Korea, and east to Japan. In the late 18th century, a Chinese *sheng* was taken west to St. Petersburg, Russia. Musicologists consider this instrument the inspiration

Above: Bamboo clarinet played inside gourd for increased resonance *Artwork by Romey Benton*

Left: Gourd bell over membrane *Artwork by Romey Benton*

Bamboo saxophone with gourd bell *Artwork and photo by Angel Sanpedro del Rio*

M'buat from Vietnam *Photo by Phong Nguyen*

for the harmonium, accordion, and harmonica—all free-reed instruments that appeared after that time.

The basic structure consists of a small windchest, often a gourd, into which are secured three to 16 bamboo pipes of varying lengths that may extend through both sides of the gourd. In the *sheng* and the *sho*, the pipes penetrate the top of the windchest but do not extend below. In the *khaen*, the pipes extend completely through the windchest and approximately one foot beyond. Each bamboo pipe contains a free reed and produces one note. The reed itself is often carved from bamboo. The instrument is played by blowing into the gourd or air reservoir and fingering holes on the bamboo pipes. The air enters the pipes, and if a hole in the side of the pipe is plugged, the reed vibrates and creates a sound. The instrument is held with the pipes directed upward by cupping the windchest loosely in the palms of the hands so that the fingertips extend up to cover the holes on the sides of the pipes. The pipes are arranged in such a way that melody and chords can be played easily and at the same time. Since the reeds can be set in motion by either inhaling or exhaling, there is continuous sound. A drone is frequently created by covering one of the side holes with wax.

The instrument continues to be made and played in many mountain communities in Southeast Asia, in a very simple form with few reeds mounted in a gourd mouthpiece. The *farood* in Borneo is one such example, with no more than five pipes. In the Abor and Assam hills of India, where the instrument is known as *khunj* or *rusen*, five to nine reeds are fitted into the gourd. In the mountains of Vietnam, Cambodia, and Thailand, it is called a *naw*.

By comparison, the *sheng* (China), *sho* (Japan), and *khaen* of the Laotian aristocracy were adapted by the court musicians, so the shape and size of the instru-

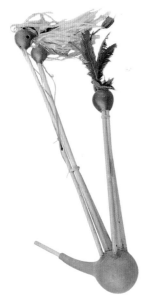

"*Rosem*." This free-reed instrument has six bamboo pipes with bamboo or metal free reeds. The long pipes contain a tuning hole covered by a gourd resonator to keep it at the same relative pitch as a shorter pipe. Chiru tribes of Manipur (northeastern India). *Courtesy of Mutua Museum, Manipur Photo by Lai Imo*

"Found in southern China and in the mountains of northern Southeast Asia, the *naw* or *hulusheng* (which literally means gourd *sheng*) is perhaps one of the oldest of the *sheng* family. It is played by the 'Hill Tribes' or minority peoples of the region, including the Lahu and Lisu peoples. It has five pipes grouped in a circular cluster whose open ends appear flush with the bottom of the gourd wind chamber, which allows the player to 'bend' the notes by slowly covering the ends of the pipes with the right thumb while playing. The technique of this instrument is difficult and the resulting music is very lively and quite loud in spite of the bamboo reeds. Traditionally this instrument also played a coded language which was used for conversation between unmarried people."—Randy Raine-Reusch *Naw from the collection of Darrel Devore*

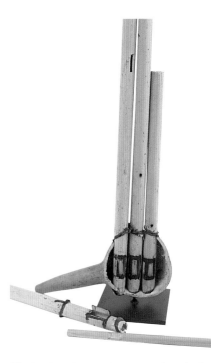

The bamboo free reeds are sealed inside the windchest. Compare this with the detail of the bamboo *naw* reed and brass *khaen* reed in the foreground. The slot visible on the tube effectively shortens the fundamental. The additional height of the tube is aesthetic. The single hole drilled into the tube just above the windchest must be closed in order for that reed to sound. "The small brass or silver reed is traditionally made by hammering a small coin on an elephant thigh bone until it is paper thin and then cut to size."—Randy Raine-Reusch

"The *sumpoton* is the free-reed mouth organ of Sabah, in northeastern Borneo. With the introduction of Christianity to the peoples of Sabah, bamboo bands became popular. These were orchestras of local instruments adapted to play religious music. This instrument has each set of three pipes tuned to major or minor chords that are grouped in a frame. This enables a musician to play a chordal melody by simply blowing on the appropriate instrument. No fingering is required as there are no fingerholes." *Randy Raine-Reusch Photo by Randy Raine-Reusch*

ment underwent many changes. The number of tubes varies from 13 in the *sho*, and 13 or 14 in the *khaen*, to 17 in the *sheng*. The gourd mouthpiece has largely been replaced today by carved wood and even metal boxes. The graduated sizes of pipes create different notes. In general, they are aligned in two rows, going from shorter to taller along both sides of the resonator.

The ancient Chinese likened the instrument to a phoenix with its wings folded upward.

The *sheng* is still played in China today, in classical operas and in popular folk music.

The *sho* in Japan consists of 13 bamboo pipes and is used primarily to play traditional music in the palace or large temples in ensemble with flutes and zithers. The oldest examples of the instrument in Japan were found in a vault of 45 ancient instruments that date from 756 A.D. Today, contemporary musicians are exploring the sound of the *sho* in combination with new instruments to reintroduce this once popular music.

In Thailand and Laos, the *khaen* is played regularly both for traditional and folk music. The bamboo tubes of the *khaen* are much longer than the *sho* or *sheng,* the longest sometimes reaching four feet beyond the windchest. The windchest is frequently carved from the roots of trees, and the reeds are now made of brass strips instead of bamboo. The *khaen* is made in four popular sizes, but the standard size is 16 pipes or eight pairs. The instrument is tuned to a seven-step octave, similar to Western tuning, with a full two-octave range. None of the music is written down, and the entire tradition, including making and playing, is learned through apprenticeship to a master musician, usually a man in the village.

Double Reeds

Mouthpieces with double reeds consist of two reeds held close together at the entrance to a narrow air channel, as in conventional oboes and bassoons. Consider purchasing an oboe mouthpiece from a music store and fitting it to a gourd body before attempting to make your own. Many instruments with a double mouthpiece attached to a gourd bell/resonator are popular in Southeast Asia.

Aeolian Instruments

Aeolian instruments are aerophones that are powered not by human breath but by the wind. Aeolian instruments can have an enclosed air chamber or no air chamber at all.

When an air chamber is present, the air movement across the opening can come from:

1. the natural wind passing a stationary gourd that has been aligned so that its sharp edge faces into the wind at the proper angle (gourd wind organ)
2. still air surrounding a sharp edge cutting into a rapidly spinning gourd (humming gourd top)
3. still air passing across a sharp edge cutting into a resonator as it is spun rapidly around in a circle on the end of a long string (*oe'oe*)
4. the laminar flow of wind off a sail or kite, directed at a sharp edge (kite flute)
5. the natural air passing across the sharp edge of a pigeon flute as the bird flies through the air (pigeon flute)

Aeolian instruments without an enclosed air chamber that can be made from a gourd fragment are the bull roarer and the spinning buzzer.

For all of the following instruments, clean the inside of the gourd by soaking

Double reed, gourd bell

Rare photo of pigeons aloft with gourd whistles attached

it in water for several days, remove the inside pulp and seeds, and then allow it to dry thoroughly for a week.

Wind Organ

Wind organ *Artwork by Ginger Summit*

Make a wind organ using a long snake or trough gourd. Cut a vertical vent in the middle of the gourd about a quarter of the length of the gourd and ⅜ inch wide, making sure to choose an area that is flat and in the same plane. Clean out the gourd by cutting a hole in the bottom, making sure to keep the plug to replace later. With a long-handled scraper, scrape and smooth the inside of the gourd. Use a knife or a small, flat rasp or file to angle the vertical cuts inward so that there is a knife edge along the two sides of the vent.

It is possible to test the cut by holding the gourd out a car window, the vent facing into the wind, while someone else drives. Keep orienting the gourd until you hear a steady drone. Experiment by cutting the vent longer and sharpening the edges. The edges must be perfectly straight and parallel. It may be necessary to widen the vent as well.

Once the vent is singing, hang the gourd vertically and attach a wind vane to it so the vane is tangent to one of the knife-edge sides of the vent. The wind vane will face the gourd into the wind at the proper angle so the wind will strike the leading edge of the vent.

Humming Gourd Top

Humming gourd top *Artwork and photo by Uli Wahl*

The humming gourd top is made from an ornamental gourd that is about two to three inches in diameter and as round and symmetrical as possible. Carefully cut the top off the gourd and clean out the inside of the gourd by scraping and lifting out the seed pack. Scrape the sides smooth, then glue the top back onto the gourd.

When the glue has dried, insert a needle into the center of the top of the gourd and another needle into the center of the bottom of the gourd. Pick up the gourd by the needles, making sure that they line up and that the gourd rotates evenly when you spin the two needles between your fingers. Keep adjusting the needles until you find the exact point where the gourd rotates symmetrically. Now spin it once again and place a pencil next to the center line of the spinning gourd and mark that point that tends to stick out a little more than the rest of the gourd. This eccentric point will be the location of the sound hole.

At the marked point for the sound hole, cut a rectangle so it is in a vertical position when the gourd is balanced on one of the two needles. The ratio of width to length should be about 1:3. Start small and slowly enlarge the rectangle until you get the best sounding results, keeping the ratio of 1:3. The vertical edges should be sharpened as in the previous project.

Readjust the needles until the gourd spins symmetrically. Mark the needle holes. Use a ¹⁄₆₄-inch drill bit and drill straight into the gourd at both ends. Push a long bamboo skewer through the holes so it emerges ¼–⅜ of an inch at the bottom of the gourd. Enlarge the hole slightly if necessary. Sand the ends of the skewer round, not pointed, and glue the skewer into place.

Try spinning the top by quickly twisting the upper section of bamboo. If the top wobbles and doesn't spin, add a little melted beeswax to the gourd to give it more mass. After adding wax, you'll probably have to balance the top again by moving the wax around. You can also press beeswax around the bottom of the gourd. Another way to spin the top is to wrap a string tightly around the handle. Throw the top onto its point while holding one end of the string and snapping the string vigorously. As the top leaves the hand and the string unfurls, it will put a spin on the top. If it lands properly, your top will spin for a long time. This technique takes a lot of practice to perfect.

Oe'oe

The *oe'oe* is a Hawaiian instrument similar to the Hawaiian nose flute, except that it is whirled around the player by an attached string. Once again, the gourd needs to be symmetrical and needs to be cleaned out thoroughly. In order to work, the *oe'oe* must have a hole at both ends. The upper hole is to accommodate a string. The lower hole will catch the wind and cause the vibrations. The additional holes in the side of the flute (the fingered holes for the nose flute) are necessary for the acoustics to work properly. The hole in the bottom of the flute must be drilled very carefully because the walls need to be perfectly straight and sharp for the cutting edge into the wind. The sound of the *oe'oe* will be soft but clearly distinguishable. The *oe'oe* is occasionally used as an accompaniment in hula.

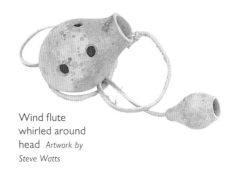

Wind flute whirled around head *Artwork by Steve Watts*

Kite Flute and Pigeon Flute

According to Wang Shixiang, the earliest record for pigeon whistles is dated 1041–1044 for military use. Otherwise, the earliest mention of the pigeon flute is in the "Sonnets of Peking," composed about 300 years ago. The author speaks of "little wooden flutes attached" to the tails of pigeons and "when set off make a lovely musical tune." The kite flute and the pigeon flute are very closely related. They are both made from small, ornamental gourds (lighter weight than Lagenaria) constructed by cutting off the top and fitting the gourd with a top into which "flute lips" have been carved. Sometimes a cardboard or bamboo wall is glued into the gourd to make two different-sized chambers and the top is then fitted with two sets of "flute lips" next to each other so that both sides of the gourd will have different pitches.

The pigeon flute differs from the kite flute in that a bone or wooden knob is attached to the bottom of the pigeon flute. The knob has a hole drilled through it that is parallel to the sound slot. To attach the flute to the pigeon, the base of the two middle tail feathers of the pigeon are tied together with string or a rubber band at the very base of the tail, and again about half an inch farther out. The knob of the flute is pushed into the slot between the two ties and

Kite flute *Artwork by Uli Wahl*

Pigeon flutes *Artwork and photo by Wang Shixiang*

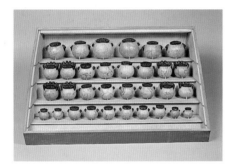

A full scale of pigeon whistles *Artwork and photo by Wang Shixiang*

Pigeon with attached flute

anchored by putting a short piece of bamboo or quill through the hole. A couple of extra ties to keep the anchor piece in place complete the installation. The gourd flute rests above the tail, on the bird's rump, with the windward edge of the slot facing forward. When the pigeon takes off and flies, the wind flowing over the bird and striking the slot causes the flute to sing continuously.

The kite flute is tied to the kite by means of a netting that is woven around the flute. The flute is mounted with its bottom on the kite and the slots pointing toward the top of the kite. Additional support ties are connected to the netting near the top of the flute. The orientation of the windward edge of the kite flute's slot is toward the laminar air flow that flows down the actual face of the kite. The laminar air flow causes the flute to sing.

Sellers of pigeon flutes test their wares by running a six-foot-long string through the hole in the knob and securely holding one end of the string in each hand. By spinning the string as you would wind up a buzzing disk, with the windward edge facing the direction of spin, the flute is spun round and round and the tone is very audible. A screw eye can be attached to the bottom of a kite flute so the hole in the eye is parallel to the slot. The flute is then spun to test it. Make sure the top and knob are securely mounted and the glue is dry before undertaking this test.

1. To make the pigeon or kite flute, choose a pear-shaped ornamental gourd with a diameter of two to three inches. The gourd wall must be "wood-hard." Scrape off the dry outer skin, then cut off the upper third of the gourd so that it is flat across. Carefully peel up the pulp and seeds from the inside. Clean the inside of the gourd thoroughly. Sand the opening flat.
2. To make the top with its "flute lips," take a thin board (lath) or slice of the outer section of a piece of bamboo a little wider than the opening of the gourd. Scrape, plane, or sand the wood flat to a thickness of ¼–⅜ inch.
3. Turn the gourd over and mark the opening onto the lath. Into this circle draw another circle with a radius of ³⁄₁₆ inch less than the outer circle. (This is to allow for the taper that you will later sand at the edge of the top.) Transfer this smaller circle onto the other side of the lath. The larger circle later will become the up side. The smaller circle will become the under part of the flute head and will be inside the flute. (Fig. 1)

Pigeon flute collection of Steve Klausner, Dove's Flight

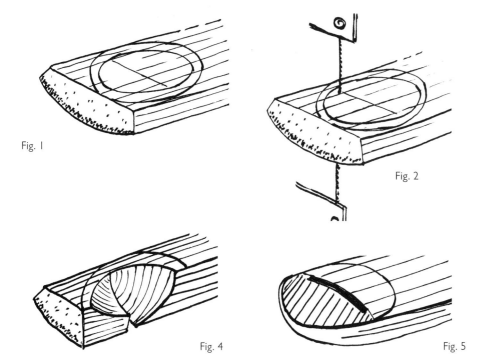

Fig. 1

Fig. 2

Fig. 3

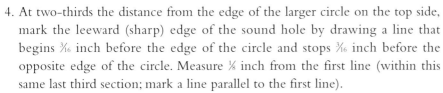

Fig. 4

Fig. 5

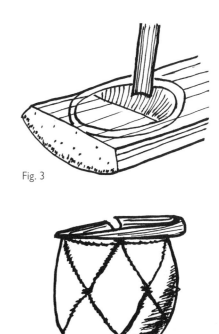

Fig. 6. The airstream moves from left to right to strike a sharp edge, thereby producing a tone.

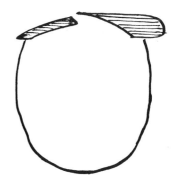

Fig. 7. Cross-section of Fig. 6.

4. At two-thirds the distance from the edge of the larger circle on the top side, mark the leeward (sharp) edge of the sound hole by drawing a line that begins ³⁄₁₆ inch before the edge of the circle and stops ³⁄₁₆ inch before the opposite edge of the circle. Measure ⅛ inch from the first line (within this same last third section; mark a line parallel to the first line).

5. Drill a small hole between these two lines at the start of the lines to allow for a thin saw blade to pass. (Fig. 2)

6. Pull a jigsaw blade through the hole and cut along the line to the other end. Make just one cut, between the two lines.

7. Begin beveling the flute head by starting at the windward edge of the circle to the sound hole saw cut. Be very careful not to damage the leeward edge of the saw cut. (Fig. 3)

8. Turn the lath over again, and carve out the leeward side of the saw cut to an angle of about 45 degrees. (Fig. 4)

9. Turn the lath over so that the top side is up, and saw out the circle from the lath. Then sand the taper along the edge of the circle to meet the circle drawn on the underside and wedge into the flute body. (Fig. 5)

10. It is difficult to test the tone of the flute until the top is glued into the gourd body. Blowing across the lips of the flute will give a hint of the sound, but your breath is too turbulent to give a clear tone. The best way to test your flute would be to hold it outside the window of a moving car. Hold the flute tightly and face the lips into the airstream.

11. To complete your pigeon flute, a bone or wooden knob needs to be added to the base. First glue a short section of bamboo skewer into the bottom of

Shave the inside of the windward side of the top at a 45-degree angle. *Artwork by Uli Wahl*

Above: Detail of flute attached to kite *Artwork and photo by Uli Wahl*

Right: Kite with flutes in the air *Artwork and photo by Uli Wahl*

A kite with 30 flutes attached. The laminar air flow will come down the kite from top to bottom, striking the flute lips. The top of the kite is at the top of the picture. *Artwork and photo by Uli Wahl*

your gourd. Then after carving the knob—a flat piece of bone or wood about ¼ x ½ inch with a hole drilled through the face—file the narrow edge to fit the contour of the bottom of the gourd and drill a tiny hole into the thickness of the knob to accept the bamboo length. Glue the knob onto the bamboo skewer and push the knob flush with the gourd.

12. The kite flute has a simple net woven around it to anchor the kite at several points.

Bull Roarer and Spinning Disk

The bull roarer and the spinning disk are aeolian instruments that do not have an enclosed air chamber, but instead activate vibrations in the air that surrounds them. These objects create sound by spinning rapidly, thereby disturbing the air immediately surrounding them and creating sound waves. These are among the most ancient of instruments. Because these two instruments create just a general turbulence in the air that is not modified by a resonating chamber, the sound created is heard as noise, often described as wailing or roaring. The spinning disk and bull roarer are very easy to make from gourd fragments. Beeswax or other material needs to be added to increase its mass so that it will develop enough speed when whirled around and around.

Forms of the bull roarer have been found around the world, including Australia, North and South America, and Africa, and are believed to have been used for perhaps 25,000 years. Traditionally, bull roarers have been associated with rituals and religious events. In Australia, the sound of the bull roarer was thought to be the sound of the supernatural spirit itself. In Mali, it represented the voice of the ancestors, or the sound of the first man who encountered death. Among the Baule in Ivory Coast, the bull roarer represented the voice of the god Goli. In other parts of West Africa, it was and continues to be associated with the sound of the panther.

To make the bull roarer, cut out a long, fairly flat fragment of thick gourd about eight to 12 inches long by three inches wide. Select a relatively thick, dense gourd shell since the force of swinging may rip or crack a thin shell. Coat it thoroughly with varnish, resin, or several coats of glue to seal the surface. A coating of tissue will further strengthen the shell and provide additional weight, which may be necessary to help the instrument spin as it is twirled. Drill a hole in one end and insert a loop of string or wire. Because the noise is generated by the spinning action of the bull roarer, you may want to attach a fisherman's swivel connector to allow for unimpeded spin. Attach this to a long and strong string, up to 10 feet in length. Begin spinning the piece overhead, making sure you are in a sufficient clearing. Adjust the speed of the whirl until you get a sound. It is possible to modify the pitch slightly by changing the speed as the gourd spins through the air.

To make the spinning disk, cut a flat circle four inches in diameter out of a thick gourd fragment. With the rasp, file long (½–¾ inch) teeth in the edge of the circle so that it looks like a circular saw blade. Drill two holes ⅜ of an inch from the center of the disk on opposite sides, so that if you drew a line through the two holes the line would also pass through the center of the disk and the center would be midway between the two holes.

Pass both ends of an eight-foot-long string through the two holes, one strand into each hole. Tie the two ends together. Move the disk so that it is in the middle of the two strands and hold the string, one hand at the doubled part of the string, the other at the knot. At this point make sure there is no twist in the string. Now slowly wind up the two strings by rotating your hands in the same direction with the disk going around and around in a vertical plane in front of you. When the string is very twisted, pull your hands apart while holding the string. The disk should begin spinning rapidly. When the string no longer has a twist, the centrifugal force of the spinning disk should start winding the string up in the opposite direction. When it reaches a maximum of twist, the disk will slow and you should pull your hands apart to make it begin spinning in the opposite direction again. The sawteeth will make a buzzing sound in the air. Just keep repeating the motion for continuous play.

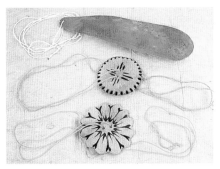

Two spinning gourd disks and a gourd bull roarer *Artwork by Ginger Summit*

Appendix
Constructing a Xylophone

Dr. Andrew Tracey, Director of the International Library of African Music, Rhodes University, in Grahamstown, South Africa, has graciously shared the following series of photographs showing the intricate step-by-step process of constructing a xylophone in Mozambique, for which the Chopi people are the undisputed masters. The care with which the gourds are precisely tuned is remarkable.

ALL THE FOLLOWING ARTWORK IS BY VENANCIO MBANDE. ALL THE FOLLOWING PHOTOS ARE BY ANDREW TRACEY.

Venancio Mbande, master Chopi *timbila* xylophone maker from Mozambique, shapes the lip of a *chibembe* gourd resonator for a *chinzumana* double-bass xylophone.

A set of prepared *matamba* gourds with a *chibembe* calabash for a low note, ready for mounting on a *sanje* alto xylophone

Venancio Mbande preparing gourd resonators for a *sanje* alto xylophone

Using a small pocket knife to open the gourd

After the inside of the gourd is cleaned, by leaving water inside until the contents soften, and has then dried for weeks, the main hole is trimmed to size and then two small holes for tying are cut on either side of it.

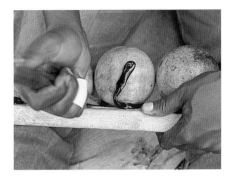

The gourds are tied with strips of *murara* palm leaf through the two small holes in the gourd to the underside of the *ditaho* frame, which has been predrilled with holes to match. The joint is then sealed with *pula,* the black wax of the ground bee, or, in this photograph, with electrician's pitch. Mr. Mbande saves his scarce beeswax for the membrane nipples and for tuning the resonators because the pitch sets much too hard. Here he is seen pressing the pitch tightly into place with a special tool called a *ponzi.*

The frame of a *sanje* alto xylophone before the keys and their supports are attached. Note the two *chibembe* gourds at the near end, because *matamba* gourds do not grow big enough for the lowest notes. The legs are held together with a temporary string so that the gourds are held off the ground.

Mr. Mbande tunes a resonator with wax/pitch. Here he is seen flattening the musical note by constricting the opening.

Looking down on top of the frame after two gourds have been attached and tuned.

On this *chinzumana* double-bass xylophone Mr. Mbande ties the gourds to the frame with strips of palm leaf before sealing with the pitch.

Sealing the large gourd to the double-bass frame with pitch

The first step in attaching the *makosi* buzzer membrane to the resonator. A red-hot poker is used to burn a hole in the side of each resonator. The high notes get smaller holes than the low notes.

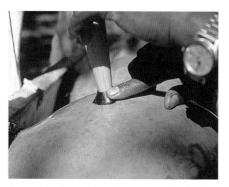

A *ponzi* tool is used as a form around which to mold the *tsudi* wax nipple, which will hold the buzzer membrane.

Partway through the process of building the *tsudi* nipples. The near gourds have not been done.

A section of *makosi* cow gut—the fine membrane covering the small intestine—is ready to be cut into a circle and attached to the *tsudi* nipple.

The *makosi* membrane is placed on its carefully preshaped nipple.

The membrane is smoothed into place with a spit-wet fingertip.

Final smooth-down of the membrane, after which it is left to dry in the sun to develop its tension

A small gourd from the *makwakwa* tree, with both its top and its bottom removed, is prepared for mounting around the membrane on the resonator to protect it.

The protective *makwakwa* gourd is sealed into place with wax.

The protective *makwakwa* gourd is sealed into place with wax—this time on the *chinzumana* double-bass.

Mr. Mbande mouth-tests a resonator for air-tightness.

Detail of the underside of the *sanje* alto xylophone showing the completed resonators

Mr. Mbande shapes a leg for the *chinzumana* double-bass xylophone. Its four large gourd resonators have been varnished and hung in the trees to dry.

Spacers are carved and decorated with an adze blade.

Tying on the "spacers" with palm leaf. These lie between every two keys and support the thongs, which in turn support the keys.

Mr. Mbande rough-shapes the sneezewood (ptaeroxylon obliquum) keys with his *chivatelo* adze before tempering.

Key blanks being tempered over hot coals in a trench

Mr. Mbande carves the top of a key to his characteristic hollow shape.

The keys gradually take shape. Sneezewood is an extremely hard and resinous wood.

The keys *(makokoma)* have been shaped. Before tuning, a square hole is burned near one end—at the nodal point.

Most of the tuning is done in the center of the key that flattens it (musically). If a key needs a little sharpening, it can be done at the ends.

The finger test on a resonator—Mr. Mbande flattens the resonator to see if it rings better that way. If so, he will add more wax to the aperture.

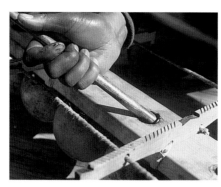

Sharpening a resonator by removing some wax

This is where a master craftsman's expertise shows. Mr. Mbande blows lightly on a resonator to check its tuning while tapping its key in the other hand for comparison. Makers in earlier times used to consider this stage critical and would do this alone, having applied much-feared *nyenze* magic ointment inside the gourd. Even now, blowing into a gourd to check its tuning is not done lightly by anybody. Mr. Mbande, a modern man, scorns the use of magic, saying that knowledge is his form of magic.

The far end of the keys shows the lacing technique.

The keys are laced differently at the near end. This end can be quickly undone during a performance and the key lifted up for running repairs to the key or resonator.

Above: Final tuning of a double-bass resonator. Mr. Mbande adjusts its aperture by hand until it sounds right, then inserts or removes wax accordingly. Note the profile of the key—thicker at the ends and thinner at the center. A xylophone key is flattened (musically) by shaving away the center.

Top left: Mr. Mbande with four *timbila* xylophones he made at the International Library of African Music at Rhodes University: a *chinzumana* double-bass, a *dibhinda* bass, and two *sanje* altos.

Middle left: Mr. Mbande checks out his new *sanje* xylophones by playing and singing some of his compositions.

Bottom left: Mr. Mbande's orchestra in full cry at a performance at Wildebeesfontein Mine, South Africa, where he worked for 40 years before retiring in 1995. The drummer only plays in one movement of the performance— *Mngeniso,* the Entry of the Dancers. The rattle player's job is to coordinate the whole line of players, which may be up to eight xylophones long in the front row. Although the Chopi rattle was originally made from a gourd, now the standard is a condensed milk can and a carved handle.

Gourd Suppliers

Dried gourds ready for crafting into musical instruments are available from the following suppliers.

Glenn Burkhalter
153 Wiljoy Rd.
Lacey's Spring, AL 35754

Darrell and Ellen Dalton
Pumpkin Hollow
610 Cr 336
Piggott, AR 72454

Jim Widess
The Caning Shop
926 Gilman St
Berkeley, CA 94710
www.caning.com

Doug and Sue Welburn
Welburn Gourd Farm
40787 Deluz Murrieta Rd.
Fallbrook CA 92028
www.welburngourdfarm.com

Roger and Kent Zittel
Zittel's Gourd Farm
6781 Oak Ave.
Folsom, CA 95630

Peter Lindberg
The Gourd Factory
Box 9
Linden, CA 95236

Tom Baal
Tree Mover Tree and Gourd Farm
5014 E. Ave N.
Palmdale, CA 93552

Walt & Donna Heer
Pumpkin and Gourd Farm
101 Creston Rd.
Paso Robles, CA 93446

Lena Braswell
Gourd Farm
1089 Hoyt Braswell Rd.
Wrens, GA 30833

Helen Thomas
Sandlady's Gourd Farm
RR 4 Box 86
Tangier, IN 47952

Bonnie Drake
6635 Old Bloomfield Rd.
Bloomfield, KY 40008

Tom Keller
PO Box 1115
West Point, MS 39773
www.enterit.com/Tom3334.htm

Kern Ackerman
Rocky Ford Gourds
Box 222
Cygnet, OH 43413

American Gourd Society
Box 274
Mt. Gilead, OH 43338-0274

John McClintock
Gourd Central
7264 SR 314
Mt. Gilead, OH 43338

Glenda Wade
221 Frankie Ln.
S. Fulton, TN 38257

West Mountain Gourd Farm
PO Box 1049
Gilmer, TX 75644

John Clark
3833 Bruce Rd.
Chesapeake, VA 23321

Australia
John Vantol
Australian Gourdfather
PO Box 298
E. Maitland
2323 NSW, Australia

Canada
Darienne McAuley
Ontario Gourd Society
272 Bland Line RR 2
Cavan, Ontario
L0A 1C0 Canada

Further information about gourds can be found at the authors' websites:
www.gingersummit.com
www.caning.com

As you explored each chapter in *Making Gourd Musical Instruments*, you found new and unusual instruments and thought to yourself, "I wonder what that sounds like."

Now you can *hear* these fascinating instruments, as well as see and create them. Ginger Summit and Jim Widess have produced an audio CD with 30 of the instruments in this book. Hearing them will give you a new appreciation for the variety and influence of gourd musical instruments and an additional incentive to build them.

The following all-gourd instruments are included on the CD:

Bro, goong, mbuat, dan bau, didgeridoo, huluse, bin, guiro, kalimba, nose flute, Native American flute, banjo, *mataphono, naw, sumpotan, keluri,* pigeon whistle, *shekere, mbira, hosho,* rainstick, *ipu heke, ulili,* xylophone, *berimbau, kora,* sitar, kite flute, clarinet, water drum, *gopiyantra, dotara,* guitar, saxophone, and ocean drum.

Featured artists are: Jai Uttal, Venancio Mbande, Orlando Hernandez, Randy Raine-Reusch, Phong Nguyen, Clarke Beuhling, Romy Benton, Russell Landers, Mehalani Uchiyama, Angel Sampedro del Rio, Cliff Walker, Steve Cervantes, Darrell Devore, Alan Perlman, Salih Qawi, Boynarr Sow, Opie O'Brien, Paul Sedgwick, Marcelo Pereira, Matt Collins, Abdi Rashid Jibril, Rene Macay, Arthur Stephens, and the Richmond Indigenous Gourd Orchestra.

The *Gourd Musical Instruments* CD is available for $12.95, postpaid, from:

The Caning Shop
926 Gilman St.
Berkeley, CA 94710-1494
1-800-544-3373   http://www.caning.com

Index

NOTE: All pages that include instructions for how to make specific instruments are in bold.

METRIC EQUIVALENTS CHART
INCHES TO MILLEMETERS AND CENTIMETERS

Inches	MM	CM	Inches	CM	Inches	CM
1/8	3	0.3	8	20.3	30	76.2
1/4	6	0.6	10	25.4	31	78.7
3/8	10	1.0	11	27.9	32	81.3
1/2	13	1.3	12	30.5	33	83.8
5/8	16	1.6	13	33.0	34	86.4
3/4	19	1.9	14	35.6	35	88.9
7/8	22	2.2	15	38.1	36	91.4
1	25	2.5	16	40.6	37	94.0
1 1/4	32	3.2	17	43.2	38	96.5
1 1/2	38	3.8	18	45.7	39	99.1
1 3/4	44	4.4	19	48.3	40	101.6
2	51	5.1	20	50.8	42	106.7
2 1/2	64	6.4	21	53.3	45	114.3
3	76	7.6	22	55.9	48	121.9
3 1/2	89	8.9	23	58.4	54	137.1
4	102	10.2	24	61.0	60	152.4
4 1/2	114	11.4	25	63.5	72	182.8
5	127	12.7	25	66.0	84	213.3
6	152	15.2	27	68.6	96	243.8